Before the Battle of Waterloo
there never was since the days of
Parises — No more firing was
heard at Brussels —

Becky admires her husband.
Rawdon (just let out of the debtors
prison) — walked home rapidly —
Rebecca dropped them there at her
husband's orders, + Lord Steyne went
away.

English Men of Letters

EDITED BY JOHN MORLEY

THACKERAY

BY

ANTHONY TROLLOPE

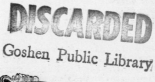
HARPER & BROTHERS PUBLISHERS

NEW YORK AND LONDON

1899

ENGLISH MEN OF LETTERS.

EDITED BY JOHN MORLEY.

12mo, Cloth, 75 cents per volume.

Other volumes in preparation.

PUBLISHED BY HARPER & BROTHERS, NEW YORK.

☞ *Any of the above works will be sent by mail, postage prepaid, to any part of the United States, Canada, or Mexico, on receipt of the price.*

CONTENTS.

CHAPTER VII.

CHAPTER VIII.

CHAPTER IX.

THACKERAY.

CHAPTER I.

BIOGRAPHICAL.

In the foregoing volumes of this series of *English Men of Letters,* and in other works of a similar nature which have appeared lately as to the *Ancient Classics* and *Foreign Classics,* biography has naturally been, if not the leading, at any rate a considerable element. The desire is common to all readers to know not only what a great writer has written, but also of what nature has been the man who has produced such great work. As to all the authors taken in hand before, there has been extant some written record of the man's life. Biographical details have been more or less known to the world, so that, whether of a Cicero, or of a Goethe, or of our own Johnson, there has been a story to tell. Of Thackeray no life has been written; and though they who knew him — and possibly many who did not — are conversant with anecdotes of the man, who was one so well known in society as to have created many anecdotes, yet there has been no memoir of his life sufficient to supply the wants of even so small a work as this purports to be. For this the reason

1*

may simply be told. Thackeray, not long before his death, had had his taste offended by some fulsome biogra‐ phy. Paragraphs, of which the eulogy seemed to have been the produce rather of personal love than of inquiry or judgment, disgusted him, and he begged of his girls that when he should have gone there should nothing of the sort be done with his name.

We can imagine how his mind had worked, how he had declared to himself that, as by those loving hands into which his letters, his notes, his little details—his literary remains, as such documents used to be called—might nat‐ urally fall, truth of his foibles and of his shortcomings could not be told, so should not his praises be written, or that flattering portrait be limned which biographers are wont to produce. Acting upon these instructions, his daughters—while there were two living, and since that the one surviving—have carried out the order which has ap‐ peared to them to be sacred. Such being the case, it cer‐ tainly is not my purpose now to write what may be called a life of Thackeray. In this preliminary chapter I will give such incidents and anecdotes of his life as will tell the reader perhaps all about him that a reader is entitled to ask. I will tell how he became an author, and will say how first he worked and struggled, and then how he work‐ ed and prospered, and became a household word in Eng‐ lish literature; how, in this way, he passed through that course of mingled failure and success which, though the literary aspirant may suffer, is probably better both for the writer and for the writings than unclouded early glory. The suffering, no doubt, is acute, and a touch of melancholy, perhaps of indignation, may be given to words which have been written while the heart has been too full of its own wrongs; but this is better than the continued note of triumph, which is still heard in the final voices of the spoilt child of literature, even when they are losing their music. Then I will tell how Thackeray died, early indeed, but still having done a good life's work. Something of his manner, something of his appearance I can say, something perhaps of his condition of mind; because for some years he was known to me. But of the continual intercourse of himself with the world, and of himself with his own works, I can tell little, because no record of his life has been made public.

William Makepeace Thackeray was born at Calcutta, on July 18, 1811. His father was Richmond Thackeray, son of W. M. Thackeray of Hadley, near Barnet, in Middlesex. A relation of his, of the same name, a Rev. Mr. Thackeray, I knew well as rector of Hadley, many years afterwards. Him I believe to have been a second cousin of our Thackeray, but I think they had never met each other. Another cousin was Provost of Kings at Cambridge, fifty years ago, as Cambridge men will remember. Clergymen of the family have been numerous in England during the century; and there was one, a Rev. Elias Thackeray, whom I also knew in my youth, a dignitary, if I remember right, in the diocese of Meath. The Thackerays seem to have affected the Church; but such was not at any period of his life the bias of our novelist's mind.

His father and grandfather were Indian civil servants. His mother was Anne Becher, whose father was also in the Company's service. She married early in India, and was only nineteen when her son was born. She was left a widow in 1816, with only one child, and was married a few years afterwards to Major Henry Carmichael Smyth, with whom Thackeray lived on terms of affectionate intercourse till the major died. All who knew William Make peace remember his mother well, a handsome, spare, gray-haired lady, whom Thackeray treated with a courtly deference as well as constant affection. There was, however, something of discrepancy between them as to matters of religion. Mrs. Carmichael Smyth was disposed to the somewhat austere observance of the evangelical section of the Church. Such, certainly, never became the case with her son. There was disagreement on the subject, and probably unhappiness at intervals, but never, I think, quarrelling. Thackeray's house was his mother's home whenever she pleased it, and the home also of his stepfather.

He was brought a child from India, and was sent early to the Charter House. Of his life and doings there his friend and school-fellow George Venables writes to me as follows:

"My recollection of him, though fresh enough, does not furnish much material for biography. He came to school young — a pretty, gentle, and rather timid boy. I think his experience there was not generally pleasant. Though he had afterwards a scholarlike knowledge of Latin, he did not attain distinction in the school; and I should think that the character of the head-master, Dr. Russell, which was vigorous, unsympathetic, and stern, though not severe, was uncongenial to his own. With the boys who knew him, Thackeray was popular; but he had no skill in games, and, I think, no taste for them. . . . He was already known by his faculty of making verses, chiefly parodies. I only remember one line of one parody on a poem of L. E. L.'s, about 'Violets, dark blue violets;' Thackeray's version was 'Cabbages, bright green cabbages,' and we thought it very witty. He took part in a scheme, which came to nothing, for a school magazine, and he wrote verses for it, of which I only remember that they were good of their

kind. When I knew him better, in later years, I thought
I could recognize the sensitive nature which he had as a
boy. . . . His change of retrospective feeling about his
school days was very characteristic. In his earlier books
he always spoke of the Charter House as Slaughter House
and Smithfield. As he became famous and prosperous his
memory softened, and Slaughter House was changed into
Grey Friars, where Colonel Newcome ended his life."

In February, 1829, when he was not as yet eighteen,
Thackeray went up to Trinity College, Cambridge, and
was, I think, removed in 1830. It may be presumed,
therefore, that his studies there were not very serviceable
to him. There are few, if any, records left of his doings
at the university—unless it be the fact that he did there
commence the literary work of his life. The line about
the cabbages, and the scheme of the school magazine, can
hardly be said to have amounted even to a commencement. In 1829 a little periodical was brought out at
Cambridge, called *The Snob*, with an assurance on the
title that it was *not* conducted by members of the university. It is presumed that Thackeray took a hand in editing this. He certainly wrote, and published in the little
paper, some burlesque lines on the subject which was
given for the Chancellor's prize poem of the year. This
was *Timbuctoo*, and Tennyson was the victor on the occasion. There is some good fun in the four first and four
last lines of Thackeray's production.

> In Africa—a quarter of the world—
> Men's skins are black; their hair is crisped and curled;
> And somewhere there, unknown to public view,
> A mighty city lies, called Timbuctoo.

＊   ＊   ＊   ＊   ＊   ＊   ＊

I see her tribes the hill of glory mount,
And sell their sugars on their own account;
While round her throne the prostrate nations come,
Sue for her rice, and barter for her rum.

I cannot find in *The Snob* internal evidence of much literary merit beyond this. But then how many great writers have there been from whose early lucubrations no future literary excellence could be prognosticated?

There is something at any rate in the name of the publication which tells of work that did come. Thackeray's mind was at all times peculiarly exercised with a sense of snobbishness. His appreciation of the vice grew abnormally, so that at last he had a morbid horror of a snob— a morbid fear lest this or the other man should turn snob on his hands. It is probable that the idea was taken from the early *Snob* at Cambridge, either from his own participation in the work or from his remembrance of it. *The Snob* lived, I think, but nine weeks, and was followed at an interval, in 1830, by *The Gownsman*, which lived to the seventeenth number, and at the opening of which Thackeray no doubt had a hand. It professed to be a continuation of *The Snob*. It contains a dedication to all proctors, which I should not be sorry to attribute to him. "To all Proctors, past, present, and future—

Whose taste it is our privilege to follow,
Whose virtue it is our duty to imitate,
Whose presence it is our interest to avoid."

There is, however, nothing beyond fancy to induce me to believe that Thackeray was the author of the dedication, and I do not know that there is any evidence to show that he was connected with *The Snob* beyond the writing of *Timbuctoo*.

In 1830 he left Cambridge, and went to Weimar either in that year or in 1831. Between Weimar and Paris he spent some portion of his earlier years, while his family— his mother, that is, and his stepfather — were living in Devonshire. It was then the purport of his life to become an artist, and he studied drawing at Paris, affecting especially Bonnington, the young English artist who had himself painted at Paris, and who had died in 1828. He never learned to draw—perhaps never could have learned. That he was idle, and did not do his best, we may take for granted. He was always idle, and only on some occasions, when the spirit moved him thoroughly, did he do his best even in after-life. But with drawing—or rather without it—he did wonderfully well even when he did his worst. He did illustrate his own books, and everyone knows how incorrect were his delineations. But as illustrations they were excellent. How often have I wished that characters of my own creating might be sketched as faultily, if with the same appreciation of the intended purpose. Let anyone look at the "plates," as they are called in *Vanity Fair*, and compare each with the scenes and the characters intended to be displayed, and there see whether the artist—if we may call him so—has not managed to convey in the picture the exact feeling which he has described in the text. I have a little sketch of his, in which a cannon-ball is supposed to have just carried off the head of an aide-de-camp—messenger I had perhaps better say, lest I might affront military feelings—who is kneeling on the field of battle and delivering a despatch to Marlborough on horseback. The graceful ease with which the duke receives the message though the messenger's head be gone, and the soldier-like precision with which the headless hero finishes his last effort of military obedience, may not have been portrayed with well-drawn figures, but no finished illustration ever told its story better. Dickens has informed us that he first met Thackeray in 1835, on which occasion the young artist aspirant, looking no doubt after profitable employment, " proposed to become the illustrator of my earliest book." It is singular that such should have been the first interview between the two great novelists. We may presume that the offer was rejected.

In 1832, Thackeray came of age, and inherited his fortune — as to which various stories have been told. It seems to have amounted to about five hundred a year, and to have passed through his hands in a year or two, interest and principal. It has been told of him that it was all taken away from him at cards, but such was not the truth. Some went in an Indian bank in which he invested it. A portion was lost at cards. But with some of it—the larger part, as I think—he endeavoured, in concert with his stepfather, to float a newspaper, which failed. There seem to have been two newspapers in which he was so concerned, *The National Standard* and *The Constitutional*. On the latter he was engaged with his stepfather, and in carrying that on he lost the last of his money. *The National Standard* had been running for some weeks when Thackeray joined it, and lost his money in it. It ran only for little more than twelve months, and then, the money having gone, the periodical came to an end. I know no road to fortune more tempting to a young man, or one that with more certainty leads to ruin. Thackeray, who in a way more or less correct, often refers in his writings, if not to the incidents, at any rate to the remembrances of his own life, tells us much of the story of this newspaper in *Lovel the Widower*. ["They are welcome," says the bachclor, "to make merry at my charges in respect of a certain bargain which I made on coming to London, and in which, had I been Moses Primrose purchasing green spectacles, I could scarcely have been more taken in. My Jenkinson was an old college acquaintance, whom I was idiot enough to imagine a respectable man. The fellow had a very smooth tongue and sleek sanctified exterior. He was rather a popular preacher, and used to cry a good deal in the pulpit. He and a queer wine-merchant and bill discounter, Sherrick by name, had somehow got possession of that neat little literary paper, *The Museum*, which perhaps you remember, and this eligible literary property my friend Honeyman, with his wheedling tongue, induced me to purchase." Here is the history of Thackeray's money, told by himself plainly enough, but with no intention on his part of narrating an incident in his own life to the public. But the drollery of the circumstances, his own mingled folly and young ambition, struck him as being worth narration, and the more forcibly as he remembered all the ins and outs of his own reflections at the time—how he had meant to enchant the world, and make his fortune. There was literary capital in it of which he could make use after so many years. Then he tells us of this ambition, and of the folly of it; and at the same time puts forward the excuses to be made for it. "I daresay I gave myself airs as editor of that confounded *Museum*, and proposed to educate the public taste, to diffuse morality and sound literature throughout the nation, and to pocket a liberal salary in return for my services. I daresay I printed my own sonnets, my own tragedy, my own verses. . . . I daresay I wrote satirical articles. . . . I daresay I made a gaby of myself to the world. Pray, my good friend, hast thou never done likewise? If thou hast never been a fool, be

sure thou wilt never be a wise man." Thackeray was
quite aware of his early weaknesses, and in the maturity
of life knew well that he had not been precociously wise.
He delighted so to tell his friends, and he delighted also
to tell the public, not meaning that any but an inner circle should know that he was speaking of himself. But
the story now is plain to all who can read.[1]

It was thus that he lost his money; and then, not having prospered very well with his drawing lessons in Paris
or elsewhere, he was fain to take up literature as a profession. It is a business which has its allurements. It
requires no capital, no special education, no training, and
may be taken up at any time without a moment's delay.
If a man can command a table, a chair, a pen, paper, and
ink, he can commence his trade as literary man. It is
thus that aspirants generally do commence it. A man
may or may not have another employment to back him,
or means of his own; or—as was the case with Thackeray,
when, after his first misadventure, he had to look about
him for the means of living — he may have nothing but
his intellect and his friends. But the idea comes to the
man that as he has the pen and ink, and time on his hand,
why should he not write and make money?

It is an idea that comes to very many men and women,
old as well as young—to many thousands who at last are
crushed by it, of whom the world knows nothing. A man

---

[1] The report that he had lost all his money and was going to live
by painting in Paris, was still prevalent in London in 1836. Macready, on the 27th April of that year, says in his *Diary:* "At Garrick
Club, where I dined and saw the papers. Met Thackeray, who has
spent all his fortune, and is now about to settle in Paris, I believe as
an artist." But at this time he was, in truth, turning to literature
as a profession.

can make the attempt though he has not a coat fit to go out into the street with; or a woman, though she be almost in rags. There is no apprenticeship wanted. Indeed, there is no room for such apprenticeship. It is an art which no one teaches; there is no professor who, in a dozen lessons, even pretends to show the aspirant how to write a book or an article. If you would be a watchmaker, you must learn; or a lawyer, a cook, or even a housemaid. Before you can clean a horse you must go into the stable, and begin at the beginning. Even the cab-driving tiro must sit for awhile on the box, and learn something of the streets, before he can ply for a fare. But the literary beginner rushes at once at the top rung of his ladder—as though a youth, having made up his mind to be a clergyman, should demand, without preliminary steps, to be appointed Bishop of London. That he should be able to read and write is presumed, and that only. So much may be presumed of everyone, and nothing more is wanted.

In truth nothing more is wanted—except those inner lights as to which so many men live and die without having learned whether they possess them or not. Practice, industry, study of literature, cultivation of taste, and the rest, will of course lend their aid, will probably be necessary before high excellence is attained. But the instances are not to seek—are at the fingers of us all—in which the first uninstructed effort has succeeded. A boy, almost, or perhaps an old woman, has sat down and the book has come, and the world has read it, and the booksellers have been civil and have written their cheques. When all trades, all professions, all seats at offices, all employments at which a crust can be earned, are so crowded that a young man knows not where to look for the means of livelihood, is there not an attraction in this which to the self-confident must be almost invincible? The booksellers are courteous and write their cheques, but that is not half the whole? *Monstrari digito!* That is obtained. The happy aspirant is written of in newspapers, or, perhaps, better still, he writes of others. When the barrister of forty-five has hardly got a name beyond Chancery Lane, this glorious young scribe, with the first down on his lips, has printed his novel and been talked about.

The temptation is irresistible, and thousands fall into it. How is a man to know that he is not the lucky one or the gifted one? There is the table, and there the pen and ink. Among the unfortunate, he who fails altogether and from the first start is not the most unfortunate. A short period of life is wasted, and a sharp pang is endured. Then the disappointed one is relegated to the condition of life which he would otherwise have filled a little earlier. He has been wounded, but not killed, or even maimed. But he who has a little success, who succeeds in earning a few halcyon, but ah! so dangerous guineas, is drawn into a trade from which he will hardly escape till he be driven from it, if he come out alive, by sheer hunger. He hangs on till the guineas become crowns and shillings—till some sad record of his life, made when he applies for charity, declares that he has worked hard for the last year or two, and has earned less than a policeman in the streets or a porter at a railway. It is to that that he is brought by applying himself to a business which requires only a table and chair, with pen, ink, and paper! It is to that which he is brought by venturing to believe that he has been gifted with powers of imagination, creation, and expression.

The young man who makes the attempt knows that he must run the chance. He is well aware that nine must

fail where one will make his running good. So much as
that does reach his ears, and recommends itself to his com-
mon-sense. But why should it not be he as well as another? There is always some lucky one winning the
prize. And this prize when it has been won is so well
worth the winning! He can endure starvation — so he
tells himself—as well as another. He will try. But yet
he knows that he has but one chance out of ten in his favour, and it is only in his happier moments that he flatters
himself that that remains to him. Then there falls upon
him—in the midst of that labour which for its success especially requires that a man's heart shall be light, and that
he be always at his best—doubt and despair. If there be
no chance, of what use is his labor?

> Were it not better done as others use,
> To sport with Amaryllis in the shade,

and amuse himself after that fashion? Thus the very industry which alone could give him a chance is discarded.
It is so that the young man feels who, with some slight
belief in himself and with many doubts, sits down to commence the literary labor by which he hopes to live.

So it was, no doubt, with Thackeray. Such were his
hopes and his fears—with a resolution of which we can
well understand that it should have waned at times, of
earning his bread, if he did not make his fortune, in the
world of literature. One has not to look far for evidence
of the condition I have described—that it was so, Amaryl-
lis and all. How or when he made his very first attempt
in London, I have not learned; but he had not probably
spent his money without forming "press" acquaintances,
and had thus formed an aperture for the thin end of the
wedge. He wrote for *The Constitutional*, of which he

was part proprietor, beginning his work for that paper as a correspondent from Paris. For awhile he was connected with *The Times* newspaper, though his work there did not, I think, amount to much. His first regular employment was on *Fraser's Magazine*, when Mr. Fraser's shop was in Regent Street, when Oliver Yorke was the presumed editor, and among contributors, Carlyle was one of the most notable. I imagine that the battle of life was difficult enough with him even after he had become one of the leading props of that magazine. All that he wrote was not taken, and all that was taken was not approved. In 1837–38, the *History of Samuel Titmarsh and the Great Hoggarty Diamond* appeared in the magazine. The *Great Hoggarty Diamond* is now known to all readers of Thackeray's works. It is not my purpose to speak specially of it here, except to assert that it has been thought to be a great success. When it was being brought out, the author told a friend of his—and of mine—that it was not much thought of at Fraser's, and that he had been called upon to shorten it. That is an incident disagreeable in its nature to any literary gentleman, and likely to be specially so when he knows that his provision of bread, certainly of improved bread and butter, is at stake. The man who thus darkens his literary brow with the frown of disapproval, has at his disposal all the loaves and all the fishes that are going. If the writer be successful, there will come a time when he will be above such frowns; but, when that opinion went forth, Thackeray had not yet made his footing good, and the notice to him respecting it must have been very bitter. It was in writing this *Hoggarty Diamond* that Thackeray first invented the name of Michael Angelo Titmarsh. Samuel Titmarsh was the writer, whereas Michael Angelo was an intending illustrator. Thackeray's nose had been broken in a school fight, while he was quite a little boy, by another little boy, at the Charter House; and there was probably some association intended to be jocose with the name of the great artist, whose nose was broken by his fellow-student Torrigiano, and who, as it happened, died exactly three centuries before Thackeray.

I can understand all the disquietude of his heart when that warning, as to the too great length of his story, was given to him. He was not a man capable of feeling at any time quite assured in his position, and when that occurred he was very far from assurance. I think that at no time did he doubt the sufficiency of his own mental qualification for the work he had taken in hand; but he doubted all else. He doubted the appreciation of the world; he doubted his fitness for turning his intellect to valuable account; he doubted his physical capacity— dreading his own lack of industry; he doubted his luck; he doubted the continual absence of some of those misfortunes on which the works of literary men are shipwrecked. Though he was aware of his own power, he always, to the last, was afraid that his own deficiencies should be too strong against him. It was his nature to be idle—to put off his work—and then to be angry with himself for putting it off. Ginger was hot in the mouth with him, and all the allurements of the world were strong upon him. To find on Monday morning an excuse why he should not on Monday do Monday's work was, at the time, an inexpressible relief to him, but had become a deep regret—almost a remorse—before the Monday was over. To such a one it was not given to believe in himself with that sturdy rock-bound foundation which we see to have belonged to some men from the earliest struggles of their

career. To him, then, must have come an inexpressible
pang when he was told that his story must be curtailed.

Who else would have told such a story of himself to
the first acquaintance he chanced to meet? Of Thackeray
it might be predicted that he certainly would do so. No
little wound of the kind ever came to him but what he
disclosed it at once. "They have only bought so many
of my new book." "Have you seen the abuse of my last
number?" "What am I to turn my hand to? They are
getting tired of my novels." "They don't read it," he
said to me of *Esmond*. "So you don't mean to publish
my work?" he said once to a publisher in an open company. Other men keep their little troubles to themselves.
I have heard even of authors who have declared how all
the publishers were running after their books; I have
heard some discourse freely of their fourth and fifth editions; I have known an author to boast of his thousands
sold in this country, and his tens of thousands in America; but I never heard anyone else declare that no one
would read his *chef-d'œuvre*, and that the world was becoming tired of him. It was he who said, when he was
fifty, that a man past fifty should never write a novel.

And yet, as I have said, he was from an early age fully
conscious of his own ability. That he was so is to be
seen in the handling of many of his early works—in *Barry Lyndon*, for instance, and the *Memoirs of Mr. C. James
Yellowplush*. The sound is too certain for doubt of that
kind. But he had not then, nor did he ever achieve that
assurance of public favour which makes a man confident
that his work will be successful. During the years of
which we are now speaking Thackeray was a literary
Bohemian in this sense—that he never regarded his own
status as certain. While performing much of the best

of his life's work he was not sure of his market, not certain of his readers, his publishers, or his price; nor was he certain of himself.

It is impossible not to form some contrast between him and Dickens as to this period of his life—a comparison not as to their literary merits, but literary position. Dickens was one year his junior in age, and at this time, viz., 1837–38, had reached almost the zenith of his reputation. *Pickwick* had been published, and *Oliver Twist* and *Nicholas Nickleby* were being published. All the world was talking about the young author who was assuming his position with a confidence in his own powers which was fully justified both by his present and future success. It was manifest that he could make, not only his own fortune, but that of his publishers, and that he was a literary hero bound to be worshipped by all literary grades of men, down to the "devils" of the printing-office. At that time Thackeray, the older man, was still doubting, still hesitating, still struggling. Everyone then had accepted the name of Charles Dickens. That of William Thackeray was hardly known beyond the circle of those who are careful to make themselves acquainted with such matters. It was then the custom, more generally than it is at present, to maintain anonymous writing in magazines. Now, if anything of special merit be brought out, the name of the author, if not published, is known. It was much less so at the period in question; and as the world of readers began to be acquainted with Jeames Yellowplush, Catherine Hayes, and other heroes and heroines, the names of the author had to be inquired for. I remember myself, when I was already well acquainted with the immortal Jeames, asking who was the writer. The works of Charles Dickens were at that time as well known to be his, and as widely read in England, as those almost of Shake-speare.

It will be said, of course, that this came from the earlier popularity of Dickens. That is of course; but why should it have been so? They had begun to make their effort much at the same time; and if there was any advantage in point of position as they commenced, it was with Thack-eray. It might be said that the genius of the one was brighter than that of the other, or, at any rate, that it was more precocious. But after-judgment has, I think, not declared either of the suggestions to be true. [I will make no comparison between two such rivals, who were so dis-tinctly different from each, and each of whom, within so very short a period, has come to stand on a pedestal so high — the two exalted to so equal a vocation. And if Dickens showed the best of his power early in life, so did Thackeray the best of his intellect. In no display of mental force did he rise above *Barry Lyndon.*] I hardly know how the teller of a narrative shall hope to mount in simply intellectual faculty above the effort there made. In what, then, was the difference? Why was Dickens already a great man when Thackeray was still a literary Bohemian?

The answer is to be found not in the extent or in the nature of the genius of either man, but in the condition of mind—which indeed may be read plainly in their works by those who have eyes to see. The one was steadfast, industrious, full of purpose, never doubting of himself, al-ways putting his best foot foremost and standing firmly on it when he got it there; with no inward trepidation, with no moments in which he was half inclined to think that this race was not for his winning, this goal not to be reached by his struggles. The sympathy of friends was good to him, but he could have done without it. The good opinion which he had of himself was never shaken by adverse criticism; and the criticism on the other side, by which it was exalted, came from the enumeration of the number of copies sold. He was a firm, reliant man, very little prone to change, who, when he had discovered the nature of his own talent, knew how to do the very best with it.

It may almost be said that Thackeray was the very opposite of this. Unsteadfast, idle, changeable of purpose, aware of his own intellect but not trusting it, no man ever failed more generally than he to put his best foot foremost. Full as his works are of pathos, full of humour, full of love and charity, tending, as they always do, to truth and honour, and manly worth and womanly modesty, excelling, as they seem to me to do, most other written precepts that I know, they always seem to lack something that might have been there. There is a touch of vagueness which indicates that his pen was not firm while he was using it. He seems to me to have been dreaming ever of some high flight, and then to have told himself, with a half-broken heart, that it was beyond his power to soar up into those bright regions. I can fancy, as the sheets went from him every day, he told himself, in regard to every sheet, that it was a failure. Dickens was quite sure of his sheets.

"I have got to make it shorter!" Then he would put his hands in his pockets, and stretch himself, and straighten the lines of his face, over which a smile would come, as though this intimation from his editor were the best joke in the world; and he would walk away, with his heart bleeding, and every nerve in an agony. There are none of us who want to have much of his work shortened now.

In 1837 Thackeray married Isabella, daughter of Colonel
Matthew Shawe, and from this union there came three
daughters, Anne, Jane, and Harriet.   The name of the
eldest, now Mrs. Richmond Ritchie, who has followed so
closely in her father's steps, is a household word to the
world of novel readers; the second died as a child; the
younger lived to marry Leslie Stephen, who is too well
known for me to say more than that he wrote, the other
day, the little volume on Dr. Johnson in this series; but
she, too, has now followed her father.   Of Thackeray's
married life what need be said shall be contained in a very
few words.   It was grievously unhappy; but the misery
of it came from God, and was in no wise due to human
fault.   She became ill, and her mind failed her.   There
was a period during which he would not believe that her
illness was more than illness, and then he clung to her and
waited on her with an assiduity of affection which only
made his task the more painful to him.   At last it became
evident that she should live in the companionship of some
one with whom her life might be altogether quiet, and she
has since been domiciled with a lady with whom she has
been happy.   Thus she was, after but a few years of married life, taken away from him, and he became, as it were,
a widower till the end of his days.

At this period, and indeed for some years after his marriage, his chief literary dependence was on *Fraser's Magazine*.   He wrote also at this time in the *New Monthly
Magazine*.   In 1840 he brought out his *Paris Sketch
Book*, as to which he tells us, by a notice printed with the
first edition, that half of the sketches had already been
published in various periodicals.   Here he used the name
Michael Angelo Titmarsh, as he did also with the *Journey
from Cornhill to Cairo*.   Dickens had called himself Boz,

and clung to the name with persistency as long as the
public would permit it. Thackeray's affection for assumed
names was more intermittent, though I doubt whether
he used his own name altogether till it appeared on the
title-page of *Vanity Fair*. About this time began his
connection with *Punch*, in which much of his best work
appeared. Looking back at our old friend as he used to
come out from week to week at this time, we can hardly
boast that we used to recognise how good the literary
pabulum was that was then given for our consumption.
We have to admit that the ordinary reader, as the ordinary
picture-seer, requires to be guided by a name. We are
moved to absolute admiration by a Raphael or a Hobbema,
but hardly till we have learned the name of the painter,
or, at any rate, the manner of his painting. I am not sure
that all lovers of poetry would recognise a *Lycidas* coming from some hitherto unknown Milton. Gradually the
good picture or the fine poem makes its way into the
minds of a slowly discerning public. *Punch*, no doubt,
became very popular, owing, perhaps, more to Leech, its
artist, than to any other single person. Gradually the
world of readers began to know that there was a speciality
of humour to be found in its pages—fun and sense, satire
and good-humour, compressed together in small literary
morsels as the nature of its columns required. Gradually
the name of Thackeray as one of the band of brethren was
buzzed about, and gradually became known as that of the
chief of the literary brothers. But during the years in
which he did much for *Punch*, say from 1843 to 1853,
he was still struggling to make good his footing in literature. They knew him well in the *Punch* office, and no
doubt the amount and regularity of the cheques from
Messrs. Bradbury and Evans, the then and still owners of

that happy periodical, made him aware that he had found for himself a satisfactory career. In "a good day for himself, the journal, and the world, Thackeray found *Punch*." This was said by his old friend Shirley Brooks, who himself lived to be editor of the paper and died in harness, and was said most truly. *Punch* was more congenial to him, and no doubt more generous, than *Fraser*. There was still something of the literary Bohemian about him, but not as it had been before. He was still unfixed, looking out for some higher career, not altogether satisfied to be no more than one of an anonymous band of brothers, even though the brothers were the brothers of *Punch*. We can only imagine what were his thoughts as to himself and that other man, who was then known as the great novelist of the day — of a rivalry with whom he was certainly conscious. *Punch* was very much to him, but was not quite enough. That must have been very clear to himself as he meditated the beginning of *Vanity Fair*.

Of the contributions to the periodical, the best known now are *The Snob Papers* and *The Ballads of Policeman X*. But they were very numerous. Of Thackeray as a poet, or maker of verses, I will say a few words in a chapter which will be devoted to his own so-called ballads. Here it seems only necessary to remark that there was not apparently any time in his career at which he began to think seriously of appearing before the public as a poet. Such was the intention early in their career with many of our best known prose writers, with Milton, and Goldsmith, and Samuel Johnson, with Scott, Macaulay, and more lately with Matthew Arnold; writers of verse and prose who ultimately prevailed some in one direction, and others in the other. Milton and Goldsmith have been known best as poets, Johnson and Macaulay as writers of prose. But with all of them there has been a distinct effort in each art. Thackeray seems to have tumbled into versification by accident; writing it as amateurs do, a little now and again for his own delectation, and to catch the taste of partial friends. The reader feels that Thackeray would not have begun to print his verses unless the opportunity of doing so had been brought in his way by his doings in prose. And yet he had begun to write verses when he was very young;—at Cambridge, as we have seen, when he contributed more to the fame of Timbuctoo than I think even Tennyson has done—and in his early years at Paris. Here again, though he must have felt the strength of his own mingled humour and pathos, he always struck with an uncertain note till he had gathered strength and confidence by popularity. Good as they generally were, his verses were accidents, written not as a writer writes who claims to be a poet, but as though they might have been the relaxation of a doctor or a barrister.

And so they were. When Thackeray first settled himself in London, to make his living among the magazines and newspapers, I do not imagine that he counted much on his poetic powers. He describes it all in his own dialogue between the pen and the album.

"Since he," says the pen, speaking of its master, Thackeray:

> "Since he my faithful service did engage,
>   To follow him through his queer pilgrimage,
>   I've drawn and written many a line and page.
>
> "Caricatures I scribbled have, and rhymes,
>   And dinner-cards, and picture pantomimes,
>   And many little children's books at times.

> "I've writ the foolish fancy of his brain;
> The aimless jest that, striking, hath caused pain;
> The idle word that he'd wish back again.

> "I've helped him to pen many a line for bread."

It was thus he thought of his work. There had been caricatures, and rhymes, and many little children's books; and then the lines written for his bread, which, except that they were written for *Punch*, was hardly undertaken with a more serious purpose. In all of it there was ample seriousness, had he known it himself. What a tale of the restlessness, of the ambition, of the glory, of the misfortunes of a great country is given in the ballads of Peter the French drummer! Of that brain so full of fancy the pen had lightly written all the fancies. He did not know it when he was doing so, but with that word fancy he has described exactly the gift with which his brain was specially endowed. If a writer be accurate, or sonorous, or witty, or simply pathetic, he may, I think, gauge his own powers. He may do so after experience with something of certainty. But fancy is a gift which the owner of it cannot measure, and the power of which, when he is using it, he cannot himself understand. There is the same lambent flame flickering over everything he did, even the dinner-cards and the picture pantomimes. He did not in the least know what he put into those things. So it was with his verses. It was only by degrees, when he was told of it by others, that he found that they too were of infinite value to him in his profession.

The *Irish Sketch Book* came out in 1843, in which he used, but only half used, the name of Michael Angelo Titmarsh. He dedicates it to Charles Lever, and in signing the dedication gave his own name. "Laying aside," he says, "for a moment the travelling title of Mr. Titmarsh, let me acknowledge these favours in my own name, and subscribe myself, &c., &c., W. M. Thackeray." So he gradually fell into the declaration of his own identity. In 1844 he made his journey to Turkey and Egypt—*From Cornhill to Grand Cairo*, as he called it, still using the old *nom de plume*, but again signing the dedication with his own name. It was now made to the captain of the vessel in which he encountered that famous white squall, in describing which he has shown the wonderful power he had over words.

In 1846 was commenced, in numbers, the novel which first made his name well known to the world. This was *Vanity Fair*, a work to which it is evident that he devoted all his mind. Up to this time his writings had consisted of short contributions, chiefly of sketches, each intended to stand by itself in the periodical to which it was sent. *Barry Lyndon* had hitherto been the longest; but that and *Catherine Hays*, and the *Hoggarty Diamond*, though stories continued through various numbers, had not as yet reached the dignity—or at any rate the length —of a three-volume novel. But of late novels had grown to be much longer than those of the old well-known measure. Dickens had stretched his to nearly double the length, and had published them in twenty numbers. The attempt had caught the public taste, and had been pre-eminently successful. The nature of the tale as originated by him was altogether unlike that to which the readers of modern novels had been used. No plot, with an arranged catastrophe or *dénoûment*, was necessary. Some untying of the various knots of the narrative no doubt were expedient, but these were of the simplest kind, done with the view of giving an end to that which might otherwise be

2*

endless. The adventures of a *Pickwick* or a *Nickleby* required very little of a plot, and this mode of telling a story, which might be continued on through any number of pages, as long as the characters were interesting, met with approval. Thackeray, who had never depended much on his plot in the shorter tales which he had hitherto told, determined to adopt the same form in his first great work but with these changes:—That as the central character with Dickens had always been made beautiful with unnatural virtue—for who was ever so unselfish as *Pickwick*, so manly and modest as *Nicholas*, or so good a boy as *Oliver?*—so should his centre of interest be in every respect abnormally bad.

As to Thackeray's reason for this—or rather as to that condition of mind which brought about this result—I will say something in a final chapter, in which I will endeavor to describe the nature and effect of his work generally. Here it will be necessary only to declare that, such was the choice he now made of a subject in his first attempt to rise out of a world of small literary contributions, into the more assured position of the author of a work of importance. We are aware that the monthly nurses of periodical literature did not at first smile on the effort. The proprietors of magazines did not see their way to undertake *Vanity Fair*, and the publishers are said to have generally looked shy upon it. At last it was brought out in numbers—twenty-four numbers instead of twenty, as with those by Dickens—under the guardian hands of Messrs. Bradbury and Evans. This was completed in 1848, and then it was that, at the age of thirty-seven, Thackeray first achieved for himself a name and reputation through the country. Before this he had been known at *Fraser's* and at the *Punch* office. He was known at the Garrick Club, and had become individually popular among literary men in London. He had made many fast friends, and had been, as it were, found out by persons of distinction. But Jones, and Smith, and Robinson, in Liverpool, Manchester, and Birmingham, did not know him as they knew Dickens, Carlyle, Tennyson, and Macaulay — not as they knew Landseer, or Stansfeld, or Turner; not as they knew Macready, Charles Kean, or Miss Faucit. In that year, 1848, his name became common in the memoirs of the time. On the 5th of June I find him dining with Macready, to meet Sir J. Wilson, Panizzi, Landseer, and others. A few days afterwards Macready dined with him. "Dined with Thackeray, met the Gordons, Kenyons, Procters, Reeve, Villiers, Evans, Stansfeld, and saw Mrs. Sartoris and S. C. Dance, White, H. Goldsmid, in the evening." Again: "Dined with Forster, having called and taken up Brookfield, met Rintoul, Kenyon, Procter, Kinglake, Alfred Tennyson, Thackeray." Macready was very accurate in jotting down the names of those he entertained, who entertained him, or were entertained with him. *Vanity Fair* was coming out, and Thackeray had become one of the personages in literary society. In the January number of 1848 the *Edinburgh Review* had an article on Thackeray's works generally as they were then known. It purports to combine the *Irish Sketch Book*, the *Journey from Cornhill to Grand Cairo*, and *Vanity Fair* as far as it had then gone; but it does in truth deal chiefly with the literary merits of the latter. I will quote a passage from the article, as proving in regard to Thackeray's work an opinion which was well founded, and as telling the story of his life as far as it was then known:

"Full many a valuable truth," says the reviewer, "has
C   3

been sent undulating through the air by men who have lived and died unknown. At this moment the rising generation are supplied with the best of their mental aliment by writers whose names are a dead letter to the mass; and among the most remarkable of these is Michael Angelo Titmarsh, alias William Makepeace Thackeray, author of the *Irish Sketch Book*, of *A Journey from Cornhill to Grand Cairo*, of *Jeames's Diary*, of *The Snob Papers* in *Punch*, of *Vanity Fair*, &c., &c.

"Mr. Thackeray is now about thirty-seven years of age, of a good family, and originally intended for the bar. He kept seven or eight terms at Cambridge, but left the university without taking a degree, with the view of becoming an artist; and we well remember, ten or twelve years ago, finding him day after day engaged in copying pictures in the Louvre, in order to qualify himself for his intended profession. It may be doubted, however, whether any degree of assiduity would have enabled him to excel in the money-making branches, for his talent was altogether of the Hogarth kind, and was principally remarkable in the pen-and-ink sketches of character and situation, which he dashed off for the amusement of his friends. At the end of two or three years of desultory application he gave up the notion of becoming a painter, and took to literature. He set up and edited with marked ability a weekly journal, on the plan of *The Athenæum* and *Literary Gazette*, but was unable to compete successfully with such long-established rivals. He then became a regular man of letters—that is, he wrote for respectable magazines and newspapers, until the attention attracted to his contributions in *Fraser's Magazine* and *Punch* emboldened him to start on his own account, and risk an independent publication." Then follows a eulogistic and, as I think, a correct criticism on the book as far as it had gone. There are a few remarks perhaps a little less eulogistic as to some of his minor writings, *The Snob Papers* in particular; and at the end there is a statement with which I think we shall all now agree: "A writer with such a pen and pencil as Mr. Thackeray's is an acquisition of real and high value in our literature."

The reviewer has done his work in a tone friendly to the author, whom he knew[1] — as indeed it may be said that this little book will be written with the same feeling —but the public has already recognised the truth of the review generally. There can be no doubt that Thackeray, though he had hitherto been but a contributor of anonymous pieces to periodicals—to what is generally considered as merely the ephemeral literature of the month— had already become effective on the tastes and morals of readers. Affectation of finery; the vulgarity which apes good breeding but never approaches it; dishonest gambling, whether with dice or with railway shares; and that low taste for literary excitement which is gratified by mysterious murders and Old Bailey executions, had already received condign punishment from Yellowplush, Titmarsh, Fitzboodle, and Ikey Solomon. Under all those names Thackeray had plied his trade as a satirist. Though the truths, as the reviewer said, had been merely sent undulating through the air, they had already become effective.

Thackeray had now become a personage — one of the recognised stars of the literary heaven of the day. It was an honour to know him; and we may well believe that the givers of dinners were proud to have him among

[1] The article was written by Abraham Hayward, who is still with us, and was no doubt instigated by a desire to assist Thackeray in his struggle upwards, in which it succeeded.

their guests. He had opened his oyster with his pen—
an achievement which he cannot be said to have accomplished until *Vanity Fair* had come out. In inquiring
about him from those who survive him, and knew him
well in those days, I always hear the same account. "If
I could only tell you the impromptu lines which fell from
him!" "If I had only kept the drawings from his pen,
which used to be chucked about as though they were
worth nothing!" "If I could only remember the droll-
eries!" Had they been kept, there might now be many
volumes of these sketches, as to which the reviewer says
that their talent was "altogether of the Hogarth kind."
Could there be any kind more valuable? Like Hogarth,
he could always make his picture tell his story; though,
unlike Hogarth, he had not learned to draw. I have had
sent to me for my inspection an album of drawings and
letters, which, in the course of twenty years, from 1829 to
1849, were despatched from Thackeray to his old friend
Edward Fitzgerald. Looking at the wit displayed in the
drawings, I feel inclined to say that had he persisted he
would have been a second Hogarth. There is a series
of ballet scenes, in which "Flore et Zephyr" are the two
chief performers, which for expression and drollery exceed
anything that I know of the kind. The set in this book
are lithographs, which were published, but I do not remember to have seen them elsewhere. There are still
among us many who knew him well—Edward Fitzgerald
and George Venables, James Spedding and Kinglake, Mrs.
Procter—the widow of Barry Cornwall, who loved him
well—and Monckton Milnes, as he used to be, whose
touching lines written just after Thackeray's death will
close this volume, Frederick Pollock and Frank Fladgate,
John Blackwood and William Russell—and they all tell

the same story. Though he so rarely talked, as good
talkers do, and was averse to sit down to work, there were
always falling from his mouth and pen those little pearls.
Among the friends who had been kindest and dearest to
him in the days of his strugglings he once mentioned
three to me—Matthew Higgins, or Jacob Omnium, as he
was more popularly called; William Stirling, who became
Sir William Maxwell; and Russell Sturgis, who is now the
senior partner in the great house of Barings. Alas, only
the last of these three is left among us! Thackeray was
a man of no great power of conversation. I doubt
whether he ever shone in what is called general society.
He was not a man to be valuable at a dinner-table as a
good talker. It was when there were but two or three together that he was happy himself and made others happy;
and then it would rather be from some special piece of
drollery that the joy of the moment would come, than
from the discussion of ordinary topics. After so many
years his old friends remember the fag-ends of the dog-
gerel lines which used to drop from him without any
effort on all occasions of jollity. And though he could
be very sad — laden with melancholy, as I think must
have been the case with him always—the feeling of fun
would quickly come to him, and the queer rhymes would
be poured out as plentifully as the sketches were made.
Here is a contribution which I find hanging in the memory of an old friend, the serious nature of whose literary
labours would certainly have driven such lines from his
mind, had they not at the time caught fast hold of him :

> "In the romantic little town of Highbury
> My father kept a circulatin' library ;
> He followed in his youth that man immortal, who
> Conquered the Frenchmen on the plains of Waterloo.

> Mamma was an inhabitant of Drogheda,
> Very good she was to darn and to embroider.
> In the famous island of Jamaica,
> For thirty years I've been a sugar-baker;
> And here I sit, the Muses' 'appy vot'ry,
> A cultivatin' every kind of po'try."

There may, perhaps, have been a mistake in a line, but the poem has been handed down with fair correctness over a period of forty years. He was always versifying. He once owed me five pounds seventeen shillings and six-pence, his share of a dinner bill at Richmond. He sent me a cheque for the amount in rhyme, giving the proper financial document on the second half of a sheet of note-paper. I gave the poem away as an autograph, and now forget the lines. This was all trifling, the reader will say. No doubt. Thackeray was always trifling, and yet always serious. In attempting to understand his character it is necessary for you to bear within your own mind the idea that he was always, within his own bosom, encountering melancholy with buffoonery, and meanness with satire. The very spirit of burlesque dwelt within him—a spirit which does not see the grand the less because of the trav-esties which it is always engendering.

In his youthful—all but boyish—days in London, he delighted to "put himself up" at the Bedford, in Covent Garden. Then, in his early married days, he lived in Al-bion Street, and from thence went to Great Coram Street, till his household there was broken up by his wife's illness. He afterwards took lodgings in St. James's Chambers, and then a house in Young Street, Kensington. Here he lived from 1847, when he was achieving his great triumph with *Vanity Fair*, down to 1853, when he removed to a house which he bought in Onslow Square. In Young Street

there had come to lodge opposite to him an Irish gentleman, who, on the part of his injured country, felt very
angry with Thackeray. *The Irish Sketch Book* had not
been complimentary, nor were the descriptions which
Thackeray had given generally of Irishmen; and there
was extant an absurd idea that in his abominable heroine
Catherine Hayes he had alluded to Miss Catherine Hayes,
the Irish singer. Word was taken to Thackeray that this
Irishman intended to come across the street and avenge
his country on the calumniator's person. Thackeray immediately called upon the gentleman, and it is said that
the visit was pleasant to both parties. There certainly
was no blood shed.

He had now succeeded—in 1848—in making for himself a standing as a man of letters, and an income. What
was the extent of his income I have no means of saying;
nor is it a subject on which, as I think, inquiry should be
made. But he was not satisfied with his position. He
felt it to be precarious, and he was always thinking of
what he owed to his two girls. That *arbitrium popularis
auræ* on which he depended for his daily bread was not
regarded by him with the confidence which it deserved.
He did not, probably, know how firm was the hold he had
obtained of the public ear. At any rate he was anxious,
and endeavoured to secure for himself a permanent income
in the public service. He had become by this time acquainted, probably intimate, with the Marquis of Clanricarde, who was then Postmaster-General. In 1848 there
fell a vacancy in the situation of Assistant-Secretary at the
General Post-Office, and Lord Clanricarde either offered it
to him or promised to give it to him. The Postmaster-
General had the disposal of the place, but was not altogether free from control in the matter. When he made

known his purpose at the Post-Office, he was met by an assurance from the officer next under him that the thing could not be done. The services were wanted of a man who had had experience in the Post-Office; and, more-over, it was necessary that the feelings of other gentlemen should be consulted. Men who have been serving in an office many years do not like to see even a man of genius put over their heads. In fact, the office would have been up in arms at such an injustice. Lord Clanricarde, who in a matter of patronage was not scrupulous, was still a good-natured man and amenable. He attempted to be-friend his friend till he found that it was impossible, and then, with the best grace in the world, accepted the official nominee that was offered to him.

It may be said that had Thackeray succeeded in that attempt he would surely have ruined himself. No man can be fit for the management and performance of special work who has learned nothing of it before his thirty-seventh year; and no man could have been less so than Thackeray. There are men who, though they be not fit, are disposed to learn their lesson and make themselves as fit as possible. Such cannot be said to have been the case with this man. For the special duties which he would have been called upon to perform, consisting to a great extent of the maintenance of discipline over a large body of men, training is required, and the service would have suffered for awhile under any untried elderly tiro. An-other man might have put himself into harness. Thack-eray never would have done so. The details of his work after the first month would have been inexpressibly weari-some to him. To have gone into the city, and to have re-mained there every day from eleven till five, would have been all but impossible to him. He would not have done it. And then he would have been tormented by the feeling that he was taking the pay and not doing the work. There is a belief current, not confined to a few, that a man may be a Government Secretary with a generous salary, and have nothing to do. The idea is something that remains to us from the old days of sinecures. If there be now remaining places so pleasant, or gentlemen so happy, I do not know them. Thackeray's notion of his future duties was probably very vague. He would have repudiated the notion that he was looking for a sinecure, but no doubt considered that the duties would be easy and light. It is not too much to assert, that he who could drop his pearls as I have said above, throwing them wide cast without an effort, would have found his work as Assistant-Secretary at the General Post-Office to be altogether too much for him. And then it was no doubt his intention to join literature with the Civil Service. He had been taught to regard the Civil Service as easy, and had counted upon himself as able to add it to his novels, and his work with his *Punch* brethren, and to his contributions generally to the literature of the day. He might have done so, could he have risen at five, and have sat at his private desk for three hours before he began his official routine at the public one. A capability for grinding, an aptitude for continuous task work, a disposition to sit in one's chair as though fixed to it by cobbler's wax, will enable a man in the prime of life to go through the tedium of a second day's work every day; but of all men Thackeray was the last to bear the wearisome perseverance of such a life. Some more or less continuous attendance at his office he must have given, and with it would have gone *Punch* and the novels, the ballads, the burlesques, the essays, the lectures, and the monthly papers full of mingled satire and tenderness, which have left to us that Thackeray which we could so ill afford to lose out of the literature of the nineteenth century. And there would have remained to the Civil Service the memory of a disgraceful job.

He did not, however, give up the idea of the Civil Service. In a letter to his American friend, Mr. Reed, dated 8th November, 1854, he says : " The secretaryship of our Legation at Washington was vacant the other day, and I instantly asked for it; but in the very kindest letter Lord Clarendon showed how the petition was impossible. First, the place was given away. Next, it would not be fair to appoint out of the service. But the first was an excellent reason — not a doubt of it." The validity of the second was probably not so apparent to him as it is to one who has himself waited long for promotion. " So if ever I come," he continues, " as I hope and trust to do this time next year, it must be in my own coat, and not the Queen's." Certainly in his own coat, and not in the Queen's, must Thackeray do anything by which he could mend his fortune or make his reputation. There never was a man less fit for the Queen's coat.

Nevertheless he held strong ideas that much was due by the Queen's ministers to men of letters, and no doubt had his feelings of slighted merit, because no part of the debt due was paid to him. In 1850 he wrote a letter to *The Morning Chronicle*, which has since been republished, in which he alludes to certain opinions which had been put forth in *The Examiner*. " I don't see," he says, " why men of letters should not very cheerfully coincide with Mr. Examiner in accepting all the honours, places, and prizes which they can get. The amount of such as will be awarded to them will not, we may be pretty sure, im-

poverish the country much ; and if it is the custom of the
State to reward by money, or titles of honour, or stars and
garters of any sort, individuals who do the country service
—and if individuals are gratified at having 'Sir' or 'My
lord' appended to their names, or stars and ribbons hooked
on to their coats and waistcoats, as men most undoubtedly
are, and as their wives, families, and relations are—there
can be no reason why men of letters should not have the
chance, as well as men of the robe or the sword ; or why,
if honour and money are good for one profession, they
should not be good for another. No man in other call-
ings thinks himself degraded by receiving a reward from
his Government ; nor, surely, need the literary man be
more squeamish about pensions, and ribbons, and titles,
than the ambassador, or general, or judge. Every European state but ours rewards its men of letters. The
American Government gives them their full share of its
small patronage ; and if Americans, why not Englishmen?"

In this a great subject is discussed which would be too
long for these pages ; but I think that there now exists a
feeling that literature can herself, for herself, produce a
rank as effective as any that a Queen's minister can be-
stow. Surely it would be a repainting of the lily, an adding a flavour to the rose, a gilding of refined gold to create
to-morrow a Lord Viscount Tennyson, a Baron Carlyle, or
a Right Honourable Sir Robert Browning. And as for pay
and pension, the less the better of it for any profession,
unless so far as it may be payment made for work done.
Then the higher the payment the better, in literature as
in all other trades. It may be doubted even whether a
special rank of its own be good for literature, such as that
which is achieved by the happy possessors of the forty
chairs of the Academy in France. Even though they had

an angel to make the choice—which they have not—that angel would do more harm to the excluded than good to the selected.

Pendennis, Esmond, and *The Newcomes* followed *Vanity Fair*—not very quickly indeed, always at an interval of two years—in 1850, 1852, and 1854. As I purpose to devote a separate short chapter, or part of a chapter, to each of these, I need say nothing here of their special merits or demerits. *Esmond* was brought out as a whole. The others appeared in numbers. "He lisped in numbers, for the numbers came." It is a mode of pronunciation in literature by no means very articulate, but easy of production and lucrative. But though easy it is seductive, and leads to idleness. An author by means of it can raise money and reputation on his book before he has written it, and when the pang of parturition is over in regard to one part, he feels himself entitled to a period of ease because the amount required for the next division will occupy him only half the month. This to Thackeray was so alluring that the entirety of the final half was not always given to the task. His self-reproaches and bemoanings when sometimes the day for reappearing would come terribly nigh, while yet the necessary amount of copy was far from being ready, were often very ludicrous and very sad—ludicrous because he never told of his distress without adding to it something of ridicule which was irresistible, and sad because those who loved him best were aware that physical suffering had already fallen upon him, and that he was deterred by illness from the exercise of continuous energy. I myself did not know him till after the time now in question. My acquaintance with him was quite late in his life. But he has told me something of it, and I have heard from those who lived with him how continual were his sufferings. In 1854, he says in one of his letters to Mr. Reed — the only private letters of his which I know to have been published: "I am to-day just out of bed after another, about the dozenth, severe fit of spasms which I have had this year. My book would have been written but for them." His work was always going on, but though not fuller of matter — that would have been almost impossible — would have been better in manner had he been delayed neither by suffering nor by that palsying of the energies which suffering produces.

This ought to have been the happiest period of his life, and should have been very happy. He had become fairly easy in his circumstances. He had succeeded in his work, and had made for himself a great name. He was fond of popularity, and especially anxious to be loved by a small circle of friends. These good things he had thoroughly achieved. Immediately after the publication of *Vanity Fair* he stood high among the literary heroes of his country, and had endeared himself especially to a special knot of friends. His face and figure, his six feet four in height, with his flowing hair, already nearly gray, and his broken nose, his broad forehead and ample chest, encountered everywhere either love or respect; and his daughters to him were all the world—the bairns of whom he says, at the end of the *White Squall* ballad:

> "I thought, as day was breaking,
> My little girls were waking,
> And smiling, and making
> A prayer at home for me."

Nothing could have been more tender or endearing than his relations with his children. But still there was a

skeleton in his cupboard—or rather two skeletons. His
home had been broken up by his wife's malady, and his
own health was shattered. When he was writing *Pendennis*, in 1849, he had a severe fever, and then those
spasms came, of which four or five years afterwards he
wrote to Mr. Reed. His home, as a home should be, was
never restored to him—or his health. Just at that period
of life at which a man generally makes a happy exchange
in taking his wife's drawing-room in lieu of the smoking-
room of his club, and assumes those domestic ways of
living which are becoming and pleasant for matured years,
that drawing-room and those domestic ways were closed
against him. The children were then no more than ba-
bies, as far as society was concerned—things to kiss and
play with, and make a home happy if they could only
have had their mother with them. I have no doubt there
were those who thought that Thackeray was very jolly
under his adversity. Jolly he was. It was the manner
of the man to be so—if that continual playfulness which
was natural to him, lying over a melancholy which was as
continual, be compatible with jollity. He laughed, and
ate, and drank, and threw his pearls about with miraculous
profusion. But I fancy that he was far from happy. I
remember once, when I was young, receiving advice as to
the manner in which I had better spend my evenings; I
was told that I ought to go home, drink tea, and read
good books. It was excellent advice, but I found that the
reading of good books in solitude was not an occupation
congenial to me. It was so, I take it, with Thackeray.
He did not like his lonely drawing-room, and went back
to his life among the clubs by no means with contentment.

In 1853, Thackeray having then his own two girls to

provide for, added a third to his family, and adopted Amy Crowe, the daughter of an old friend, and sister of the well-known artist now among us. How it came to pass that she wanted a home, or that this special home suited her, it would be unnecessary here to tell even if I knew. But that he did give a home to this young lady, making her in all respects the same as another daughter, should be told of him. He was a man who liked to broaden his back for the support of others, and to make himself easy under such burdens. In 1862, she married a Thackeray cousin, a young officer with the Victoria Cross, Edward Thackeray, and went out to India, where she died.

In 1854, the year in which *The Newcomes* came out, Thackeray had broken his close alliance with *Punch*. In December of that year there appeared from his pen an article in *The Quarterly* on *John Leech's Pictures of Life and Character*. It is a rambling discourse on picture-illustration in general, full of interest, but hardly good as a criticism — a portion of literary work for which he was not specially fitted. In it he tells us how Richard Doyle, the artist, had given up his work for *Punch*, not having been able, as a Roman Catholic, to endure the skits which, at that time, were appearing in one number after another against what was then called Papal aggression. The reviewer — Thackeray himself — then tells us of the secession of himself from the board of brethren. "Another member of Mr. Punch's cabinet, the biographer of *Jeames*, the author of *The Snob Papers*, resigned his functions, on account of Mr. Punch's assaults upon the present Emperor of the French nation, whose anger Jeames thought it was unpatriotic to arouse." How hard it must be for Cabinets to agree! This man or that is sure to have some pet conviction of his own, and the better the man the stronger

3

the conviction! Then the reviewer went on in favour of
the artist of whom he was specially speaking, making a
comparison which must at the time have been odious
enough to some of the brethren. "There can be no
blinking the fact that in Mr. Punch's Cabinet John Leech
is the right-hand man. Fancy a number of *Punch* without Leech's pictures! What would you give for it?"
Then he breaks out into strong admiration of that one
friend—perhaps with a little disregard as to the feelings
of other friends.[1] This *Critical Review*, if it may properly be so called—at any rate it is so named as now published—is to be found in our author's collected works, in
the same volume with *Catherine*. It is there preceded by
another, from *The Westminster Review*, written fourteen
years earlier, on *The Genius of Cruikshank*. This contains a descriptive catalogue of Cruikshank's works up to
that period, and is interesting, from the piquant style in
which it is written. I fancy that these two are the only
efforts of the kind which he made—and in both he dealt
with the two great caricaturists of his time, he himself being, in the imaginative part of a caricaturist's work, equal
in power to either of them.

We now come to a phase of Thackeray's life in which
he achieved a remarkable success, attributable rather to
his fame as a writer than to any particular excellence in
the art which he then exercised. He took upon himself

[1] For a week there existed at the *Punch* office a grudge against
Thackeray in reference to this awkward question: "What would
you give for your *Punch* without John Leech?" Then he asked the
confraternity to dinner—*more Thackerayano*—and the confraternity
came. Who can doubt but they were very jolly over the little blun-
der? For years afterwards Thackeray was a guest at the well-
known *Punch* dinner, though he was no longer one of the contributors.

the functions of a lecturer, being moved to do so by a hope that he might thus provide a sum of money for the future sustenance of his children. No doubt he had been advised to this course, though I do not know from whom specially the advice may have come. Dickens had already considered the subject, but had not yet consented to read in public for money on his own account. John Forster, writing of the year 1846, says of Dickens and the then only thought-of exercise of a new profession: "I continued to oppose, for reasons to be stated in their place, that which he had set his heart upon too strongly to abandon, and which I still can wish he had preferred to surrender with all that seemed to be its enormous gain." And again he says, speaking of a proposition which had been made to Dickens from the town of Bradford: "At first this was entertained, but was abandoned, with some reluctance, upon the argument that to become publicly a reader must alter, without improving, his position publicly as a writer, and that it was a change to be justified only when the higher calling should have failed of the old success." The meaning of this was that the money to be made would be sweet, but that the descent to a profession which was considered to be lower than that of literature itself would carry with it something that was bitter. It was as though one who had sat on the Woolsack as Lord Chancellor should raise the question whether, for the sake of the income attached to it, he might, without disgrace, occupy a seat on a lower bench; as though an architect should consider with himself the propriety of making his fortune as a contractor; or the head of a college lower his dignity, while he increased his finances, by taking pupils. When such discussions arise, money generally carries the day — and should do so. When convinced that money

D 4

may be earned without disgrace, we ought to allow money
to carry the day.   When we talk of sordid gain and filthy
lucre, we are generally hypocrites.   If gains be sordid
and lucre filthy, where is the priest, the lawyer, the doctor, or the man of literature, who does not wish for dirty
hands ?   An income, and the power of putting by something for old age, something for those who are to come
after, is the wholesome and acknowledged desire of all
professional men.   Thackeray having children, and being
gifted with no power of making his money go very far,
was anxious enough on the subject.   We may say now,
that had he confined himself to his pen, he would not
have wanted while he lived, but would have left but little
behind him.   That he was anxious we have seen, by his
attempts to subsidise his literary gains by a Government
office.   I cannot but think that had he undertaken public
duties for which he was ill qualified, and received a salary
which he could hardly have earned, he would have done
less for his fame than by reading to the public.   Whether
he did that well or ill, he did it well enough for the money.   The people who heard him, and who paid for their
seats, were satisfied with their bargain—as they were also
in the case of Dickens; and I venture to say that in becoming publicly a reader, neither did Dickens or Thackeray "alter his position as a writer," and " that it was a
change to be justified," though the success of the old calling had in no degree waned.   What Thackeray did enabled him to leave a comfortable income for his children,
and one earned honestly, with the full approval of the
world around him.

Having saturated his mind with the literature of Queen
Anne's time—not probably, in the first instance, as a preparation for *Esmond*, but in such a way as to induce him

to create an Esmond—he took the authors whom he knew so well as the subject for his first series of lectures. He wrote *The English Humourists of the Eighteenth Century* in 1851, while he must have been at work on *Esmond*, and first delivered the course at Willis's Rooms in that year. He afterwards went with these through many of our provincial towns, and then carried them to the United States, where he delivered them to large audiences in the winter of 1852 and 1853. Some few words as to the merits of the composition I will endeavour to say in another place. I myself never heard him lecture, and can therefore give no opinion of the performance. That which I have heard from others has been very various. It is, I think, certain that he had none of those wonderful gifts of elocution which made it a pleasure to listen to Dickens, whatever he read or whatever he said; nor had he that power of application by using which his rival taught himself with accuracy the exact effect to be given to every word. The rendering of a piece by Dickens was composed as an oratorio is composed, and was then studied by heart as music is studied. And the piece was all given by memory, without any looking at the notes or words. There was nothing of this with Thackeray. But the thing read was in itself of great interest to educated people. The words were given clearly, with sufficient intonation for easy understanding, so that they who were willing to hear something from him felt on hearing that they had received full value for their money. At any rate, the lectures were successful. The money was made—and was kept.

He came from his first trip to America to his new house in Onslow Square, and then published *The Newcomes*. This, too, was one of his great works, as to which I shall have to speak hereafter. Then, having enjoyed his success in the first attempt to lecture, he prepared a second series. He never essayed the kind of reading which with Dickens became so wonderfully popular. Dickens recited portions from his well-known works. Thackeray wrote his lectures expressly for the purpose. They have since been added to his other literature, but they were prepared as lectures. The second series were *The Four Georges.* In a lucrative point of view they were even more successful than the first, the sum of money realised in the United States having been considerable. In England they were less popular, even if better attended, the subject chosen having been distasteful to many. There arose the question whether too much freedom had not been taken with an office which, though it be no longer considered to be founded on divine right, is still as sacred as can be anything that is human. If there is to remain among us a sovereign, that sovereign, even though divested of political power, should be endowed with all that personal respect can give. If we wish ourselves to be high, we should treat that which is over us as high. And this should not depend altogether on personal character, though we know —as we have reason to know—how much may be added to the firmness of the feeling by personal merit. The respect of which we speak should, in the strongest degree, be a possession of the immediate occupant, and will naturally become dim—or perhaps be exaggerated—in regard to the past, as history or fable may tell of them. No one need hesitate to speak his mind of King John, let him be ever so strong a stickler for the privileges of majesty. But there are degrees of distance, and the throne of which we wish to preserve the dignity seems to be assailed when unmeasured evil is said of one who has sat there within

our own memory. There would seem to each of us to be
a personal affront were a departed relative delineated with
all those faults by which we must own that even our near
relatives have been made imperfect. It is a general conviction as to this which so frequently turns the biography
of those recently dead into mere eulogy. The fictitious
charity which is enjoined by the *de mortuis nil nisi bonum*
banishes truth. The feeling of which I speak almost leads
me at this moment to put down my pen. And, if so much
be due to all subjects, is less due to a sovereign?

Considerations such as these diminished, I think, the
popularity of Thackeray's second series of lectures; or,
rather, not their popularity, but the estimation in which
they were held. On this head he defended himself more
than once very gallantly, and had a great deal to say on
his side of the question. "Suppose, for example, in America—in Philadelphia or in New York—that I had spoken
about George IV. in terms of praise and affected reverence, do you believe they would have hailed his name with
cheers, or have heard it with anything of respect?" And
again: "We degrade our own honour and the sovereign's
by unduly and unjustly praising him; and the mere slav-
erer and flatterer is one who comes forward, as it were,
with flash notes, and pays with false coin his tribute to
Cæsar. I don't disguise that I feel somehow on my trial
here for loyalty—for honest English feeling." This was
said by Thackeray at a dinner at Edinburgh, in 1857, and
shows how the matter rested on his mind. Thackeray's
loyalty was no doubt true enough, but was mixed with
but little of reverence. He was one who revered modesty
and innocence rather than power, against which he had in
the bottom of his heart something of republican tendency.
His leaning was no doubt of the more manly kind. But

in what he said at Edinburgh he hardly hit the nail on
the head. No one had suggested that he should have said
good things of a king which he did not believe to be true.
The question was whether it may not be well sometimes
for us to hold our tongues. An American literary man,
here in England, would not lecture on the morals of Hamilton, on the manners of General Jackson, on the general
amenities of President Johnson.

In 1857 Thackeray stood for Oxford, in the Liberal interest, in opposition to Mr. Cardwell. He had been induced to do this by his old friend Charles Neate, who himself twice sat for Oxford, and died now not many months
since. He polled 1,017 votes, against 1,070 by Mr. Cardwell; and was thus again saved by his good fortune from
attempting to fill a situation in which he would not have
shone. There are, no doubt, many to whom a seat in Parliament comes almost as the birthright of a well-born and
well-to-do English gentleman. They go there with no
more idea of shining than they do when they are elected
to a first-class club—hardly with more idea of being use-
ful. It is the thing to do, and the House of Commons is
the place where a man ought to be—for a certain number
of hours. Such men neither succeed nor fail, for nothing
is expected of them. From such a one as Thackeray something would have been expected, which would not have
been forthcoming. He was too desultory for regular work
—full of thought, but too vague for practical questions.
He could not have endured to sit for two or three hours at
a time with his hat over his eyes, pretending to listen, as
is the duty of a good legislator. He was a man intolerant
of tedium, and in the best of his time impatient of slow
work. Nor, though his liberal feelings were very strong,
were his political convictions definite or accurate. He was

a man who mentally drank in much, feeding his fancy
hourly with what he saw, what he heard, what he read,
and then pouring it all out with an immense power of am-
plification. But it would have been impossible for him to
study and bring home to himself the various points of a
complicated bill with a hundred and fifty clauses. In becoming a man of letters, and taking that branch of letters
which fell to him, he obtained the special place that was
fitted for him. He was a round peg in a round hole.
There was no other hole which he would have fitted nearly so well. But he had his moment of political ambition,
like others—and paid a thousand pounds for his attempt.

In 1857 the first number of *The Virginians* appeared;
and the last—the twenty-fourth—in October, 1859. This
novel, as all my readers are aware, is a continuance of *Esmond*, and will be spoken of in its proper place. He was
then forty-eight years old, very gray, with much of age
upon him, which had come from suffering—age shown by
dislike of activity and by an old man's way of thinking
about many things—speaking as though the world were
all behind him instead of before; but still with a stalwart
outward bearing, very erect in his gait, and a countenance
peculiarly expressive and capable of much dignity. I speak
of his personal appearance at this time, because it was then
only that I became acquainted with him. In 1859 he un-
dertook the last great work of his life, the editorship of
The Cornhill Magazine, a periodical set on foot by Mr.
George Smith, of the house of Smith and Elder, with an
amount of energy greater than has generally been bestowed
upon such enterprises. It will be well remembered still
how much *The Cornhill* was talked about and thought of
before it first appeared, and how much of that thinking
and talking was due to the fact that Mr. Thackeray was to

edit it. *Macmillan's*, I think, was the first of the shilling magazines, having preceded *The Cornhill* by a month, and it would ill become me, who have been a humble servant to each of them, to give to either any preference. But it must be acknowledged that a great deal was expected from *The Cornhill*, and I think it will be confessed that it was the general opinion that a great deal was given by it. Thackeray had become big enough to give a special *éclat* to any literary exploit to which he attached himself. Since the days of *The Constitutional* he had fought his way up the ladder, and knew how to take his stand there with an assurance of success. When it became known to the world of readers that a new magazine was to appear under Thackeray's editorship, the world of readers was quite sure that there would be a large sale. Of the first number over one hundred and ten thousand were sold, and of the second and third over one hundred thousand. It is in the nature of such things that the sale should fall off when the novelty is over. People believe that a new delight has come, a new joy for ever, and then find that the joy is not quite so perfect or enduring as they had expected. But the commencement of such enterprises may be taken as a measure of what will follow. The magazine, either by Thackeray's name or by its intrinsic merits — probably by both—achieved a great success. My acquaintance with him grew from my having been one of his staff from the first.

About two months before the opening day I wrote to him suggesting that he should accept from me a series of four short stories on which I was engaged. I got back a long letter in which he said nothing about my short stories, but asking whether I could go to work at once and let him have a long novel, so that it might begin with the

first number. At the same time I heard from the publisher, who suggested some interesting little details as to
honorarium. The little details were very interesting, but
absolutely no time was allowed to me. It was required
that the first portion of my book should be in the printer's
hands within a month. Now it was my theory—and ever
since this occurrence has been my practice — to see the
end of my own work before the public should see the commencement.[1] If I did this thing I must not only abandon
my theory, but instantly contrive a story, or begin to write
it before it was contrived. That was what I did, urged by
the interesting nature of the details. A novelist cannot
always at the spur of the moment make his plot and create his characters who shall, with an arranged sequence
of events, live with a certain degree of eventful decorum,
through that portion of their lives which is to be portrayed. I hesitated, but allowed myself to be allured to what
I felt to be wrong, much dreading the event. How seldom
is it that theories stand the wear and tear of practice! I
will not say that the story which came was good, but it
was received with greater favour than any I had written
before or have written since. I think that almost anything would have been then accepted coming under Thackeray's editorship.

I was astonished that work should be required in such
haste, knowing that much preparation had been made, and

---

[1] I had begun an Irish story and half finished it, which would
reach just the required length. Would that do? I asked. I was civil-
ly told that my Irish story would no doubt be charming, but was not
quite the thing that was wanted. Could I not begin a new one—
English—and if possible about clergymen? The details were so interesting that had a couple of archbishops been demanded, I should
have produced them.

that the service of almost any English novelist might have
been obtained if asked for in due time. It was my readiness that was needed, rather than any other gift! The
riddle was read to me after a time. Thackeray had himself intended to begin with one of his own great novels,
but had put it off till it was too late. *Lovel the Widower*
was commenced at the same time with my own story, but
Lovel the Widower was not substantial enough to appear
as the principal joint at the banquet. Though your guests
will undoubtedly dine off the little delicacies you provide
for them, there must be a heavy saddle of mutton among
the viands prepared. I was the saddle of mutton, Thackeray having omitted to get his joint down to the fire in time
enough. My fitness lay in my capacity for quick roasting.

It may be interesting to give a list of the contributors
to the first number. My novel called *Framley Parsonage*
came first. At this banquet the saddle of mutton was
served before the delicacies. Then there was a paper by
Sir John Bowring on *The Chinese and Outer Barbarians.*
The commencing number of *Lovel the Widower* followed.
George Lewes came next with his first chapters of *Studies
in Animal Life.* Then there was Father Prout's *Inaugu-
ration Ode,* dedicated to the author of *Vanity Fair* —
which should have led the way. I need hardly say that
Father Prout was the Rev. F. Mahony. Then followed *Our
Volunteers,* by Sir John Burgoyne; *A Man of Letters of the
Last Generation,* by Thornton Hunt; *The Search for Sir
John Franklin,* from a private journal of an officer of the
Fox, now Sir Allen Young; and *The First Morning of*
1860, by Mrs. Archer Clive. The number was concluded
by the first of those *Roundabout Papers* by Thackeray
himself, which became so delightful a portion of the litera-
ture of *The Cornhill Magazine.*

It would be out of my power, and hardly interesting, to give an entire list of those who wrote for *The Cornhill* under Thackeray's editorial direction. But I may name a few, to show how strong was the support which he received. Those who contributed to the first number I have named. Among those who followed were Alfred Tennyson, Jacob Omnium, Lord Houghton, William Russell, Mrs. Beecher Stowe, Mrs. Browning, Robert Bell, George Augustus Sala, Mrs. Gaskell, James Hinton, Mary Howitt, John Kaye, Charles Lever, Frederick Locker, Laurence Oliphant, John Ruskin, Fitzjames Stephen, T. A. Trollope, Henry Thompson, Herman Merivale, Adelaide Proctor, Matthew Arnold, the present Lord Lytton, and Miss Thackeray, now Mrs. Ritchie. Thackeray continued the editorship for two years and four months, namely, up to April, 1862; but, as all readers will remember, he continued to write for it till he died, the day before Christmas Day, in 1863. His last contribution was, I think, a paper written for and published in the November number, called "*Strange to say on Club Paper*," in which he vindicated Lord Clyde from the accusation of having taken the club stationery home with him. It was not a great subject, for no one could or did believe that the Field-Marshal had been guilty of any meanness; but the handling of it has made it interesting, and his indignation has made it beautiful.

The magazine was a great success, but justice compels me to say that Thackeray was not a good editor. As he would have been an indifferent civil servant, an indifferent member of Parliament, so was he perfunctory as an editor. It has sometimes been thought well to select a popular literary man as an editor; first, because his name will attract, and then with an idea that he who can write well himself will be a competent judge of the writings of oth-

crs. The first may sell a magazine, but will hardly make
it good; and the second will not avail much, unless the
editor so situated be patient enough to read what is sent
to him. Of a magazine editor it is required that he should
be patient, scrupulous, judicious, but above all things hard-
hearted. I think it may be doubted whether Thackeray
did bring himself to read the basketfuls of manuscripts
with which he was deluged, but he probably did, sooner or
later, read the touching little private notes by which they
were accompanied—the heartrending appeals, in which he
was told that if this or the other little article could be
accepted and paid for, a starving family might be saved
from starvation for a month. He tells us how he felt on
receiving such letters in one of his *Roundabout Papers*,
which he calls "*Thorns in the cushion*." "How am I to
know," he says—"though to be sure I begin to know now
—as I take the letters off the tray, which of those enve-
lopes contains a real *bona fide* letter, and which a thorn?
One of the best invitations this year I mistook for a thorn
letter, and kept it without opening." Then he gives the
sample of a thorn letter. It is from a governess with
a poem, and with a prayer for insertion and payment.
"We have known better days, sir. I have a sick and
widowed mother to maintain, and little brothers and sis-
ters who look to me." He could not stand this, and the
money would be sent, out of his own pocket, though the
poem might be—postponed, till happily it should be lost.

From such material a good editor could not be made.
Nor, in truth, do I think that he did much of the editorial
work. I had once made an arrangement, not with Thackeray, but with the proprietors, as to some little story. The
story was sent back to me by Thackeray—rejected. *Virginibus puerisque!* That was the gist of his objection.

There was a project in a gentleman's mind — as told in my story — to run away with a married woman! Thackeray's letter was very kind, very regretful—full of apology for such treatment to such a contributor. But— *Virginibus puerisque!* I was quite sure that Thackeray had not taken the trouble to read the story himself. Some moral deputy had read it, and disapproving, no doubt properly, of the little project to which I have alluded, had incited the editor to use his authority. That Thackeray had suffered when he wrote it was easy to see, fearing that he was giving pain to one he would fain have pleased. I wrote him a long letter in return, as full of drollery as I knew how to make it. In four or five days there came a reply in the same spirit—boiling over with fun. He had kept my letter by him, not daring to open it—as he says that he did with that eligible invitation. At last he had given it to one of his girls to examine—to see whether the thorn would be too sharp, whether I had turned upon him with reproaches. A man so susceptible, so prone to work by fits and starts, so unmethodical, could not have been a good editor.

In 1862 he went into the new house which he had built for himself at Palace Green. I remember well, while this was still being built, how his friends used to discuss his imprudence in building it. Though he had done well with himself, and had made and was making a large income, was he entitled to live in a house the rent of which could not be counted at less than from five hundred to six hundred pounds a year? Before he had been there two years, he solved the question by dying — when the house was sold for two thousand pounds more than it had cost. He himself, in speaking of his project, was wont to declare that he was laying out his money in the best way he could

for the interest of his children; and it turned out that
he was right.

In 1863 he died in the house which he had built, and
at the period of his death was writing a new novel in
numbers, called *Denis Duval.* In *The Cornhill, The Adventures of Philip* had appeared. This new enterprise
was destined for commencement on 1st January, 1864,
and, though the writer was gone, it kept its promise, as far
as it went. Three numbers, and what might probably
have been intended for half of a fourth, appeared. It
may be seen, therefore, that he by no means held to my
theory, that the author should see the end of his work before the public sees the commencement. But neither did
Dickens or Mrs. Gaskell, both of whom died with stories
not completed, which, when they died, were in the course
of publication. All the evidence goes against the necessity of such precaution. Nevertheless, were I giving advice to a tiro in novel writing, I should recommend it.

With the last chapter of *Denis Duval* was published in
the magazine a set of notes on the book, taken for the
most part from Thackeray's own papers, and showing how
much collateral work he had given to the fabrication of
his novel. No doubt in preparing other tales, especially
Esmond, a very large amount of such collateral labour was
found necessary. He was a man who did very much of
such work, delighting to deal in little historical incidents.
They will be found in almost everything that he did, and
I do not know that he was ever accused of gross mistakes.
But I doubt whether on that account he should be called
a laborious man. He could go down to Winchelsea, when
writing about the little town, to see in which way the
streets lay, and to provide himself with what we call local
colouring. He could jot down the suggestions, as they

came to his mind, of his future story. There was an ir-
regularity in such work which was to his taste. His very
notes would be delightful to read, partaking of the nature
of pearls when prepared only for his own use. But he
could not bring himself to sit at his desk and do an allot-
ted task day after day. He accomplished what must be
considered as quite a sufficient life's work. He had about
twenty-five years for the purpose, and that which he has
left is an ample produce for the time. Nevertheless he
was a man of fits and starts, who, not having been in his
early years drilled to method, never achieved it in his career.

He died on the day before Christmas Day, as has been
said above, very suddenly, in his bed, early in the morning,
in the fifty-third year of his life. To those who saw him
about in the world there seemed to be no reason why he
should not continue his career for the next twenty years.
But those who knew him were so well aware of his constant sufferings, that, though they expected no sudden catastrophe, they were hardly surprised when it came. His
death was probably caused by those spasms of which he
had complained ten years before, in his letter to Mr. Reed.
On the last day but one of the year, a crowd of sorrowing
friends stood over his grave as he was laid to rest in Ken-
sal Green; and, as quickly afterwards as it could be exe-
cuted, a bust to his memory was put up in Westminster
Abbey. It is a fine work of art, by Marochetti; but, as a
likeness, is, I think, less effective than that which was mod-
elled, and then given to the Garrick Club, by Durham, and
has lately been put into marble, and now stands in the upper vestibule of the club. Neither of them, in my opinion,
give so accurate an idea of the man as a statuette in bronze,
by Boehm, of which two or three copies were made. One
of them is in my possession. It has been alleged, in refer-

ence to this, that there is something of a caricature in the
lengthiness of the figure, in the two hands thrust into the
trousers pockets, and in the protrusion of the chin. But
this feeling has originated in the general idea that any
face, or any figure, not made by the artist more beautiful
or more graceful than the original is an injustice. The
face must be smoother, the pose of the body must be more
dignified, the proportions more perfect, than in the person
represented, or satisfaction is not felt. Mr. Boehm has
certainly not flattered, but, as far as my eye can judge, he
has given the figure of the man exactly as he used to stand
before us. I have a portrait of him in crayon, by Samuel
Lawrence, as like, but hardly as natural.

A little before his death Thackeray told me that he had
then succeeded in replacing the fortune which he had lost
as a young man. He had, in fact, done better, for he left
an income of seven hundred and fifty pounds behind him.

It has been said of Thackeray that he was a cynic.
This has been said so generally, that the charge against
him has become proverbial. This, stated barely, leaves
one of two impressions on the mind, or perhaps the two
together—that this cynicism was natural to his character
and came out in his life, or that it is the characteristic of
his writings. Of the nature of his writings generally, I
will speak in the last chapter of this little book. As to
his personal character as a cynic, I must find room to
quote the following first stanzas of the little poem which
appeared to his memory in *Punch*, from the pen of Shirley Brooks:

> He was a cynic! By his life all wrought
>   Of generous acts, mild words, and gentle ways;
> His heart wide open to all kindly thought,
>   His hand so quick to give, his tongue to praise!

He was a cynic!   You might read it writ
    In that broad brow, crowned with its silver hair,
In those blue eyes, with childlike candour lit,
    In that sweet smile his lips were wont to wear!

He was a cynic!   By the love that clung
    About him from his children, friends, and kin;
By the sharp pain light pen and gossip tongue
    Wrought in him, chafing the soft heart within!

The spirit and nature of the man have been caught here
with absolute truth.   A public man should of course be
judged from his public work.   If he wrote as a cynic—a
point which I will not discuss here—it may be fair that
he who is to be known as a writer should be so called.
But, as a man, I protest that it would be hard to find an
individual farther removed from the character.   Over and
outside his fancy, which was the gift which made him so
remarkable—a certain feminine softness was the most remarkable trait about him.   To give some immediate pleasure was the great delight of his life — a sovereign to a
schoolboy, gloves to a girl, a dinner to a man, a compliment to a woman.   His charity was overflowing.   His
generosity excessive.   I heard once a story of woe from a
man who was the dear friend of both of us.   The gentleman wanted a large sum of money instantly—something
under two thousand pounds—had no natural friends who
could provide it, but must go utterly to the wall without
it.   Pondering over this sad condition of things just re-
vealed to me, I met Thackeray between the two mounted
heroes at the Horse Guards, and told him the story.   "Do
you mean to say that I am to find two thousand pounds?"
he said, angrily, with some expletives.   I explained that
I had not even suggested the doing of anything — only
that we might discuss the matter.   Then there came over

E   5

his face a peculiar smile, and a wink in his eye, and he whispered his suggestion, as though half ashamed of his meanness. "I'll go half," he said, "if anybody will do the rest." And he did go half, at a day or two's notice, though the gentleman was no more than simply a friend. I am glad to be able to add that the money was quickly repaid. I could tell various stories of the same kind, only that I lack space, and that they, if simply added one to the other, would lack interest.

He was no cynic, but he was a satirist, and could now and then be a satirist in conversation, hitting very hard when he did hit. When he was in America, he met at dinner a literary gentlemen of high character, middle-aged, and most dignified deportment. The gentleman was one whose character and acquirements stood very high—deservedly so—but who, in society, had that air of wrapping his toga around him, which adds, or is supposed to add, many cubits to a man's height. But he had a broken nose. At dinner he talked much of the tender passion, and did so in a manner which stirred up Thackeray's feeling of the ridiculous. "What has the world come to," said Thackeray, out loud to the table, "when two broken-nosed old fogies like you and me sit talking about love to each other!" The gentleman was astounded, and could only sit wrapping his toga in silent dismay for the rest of the evening. Thackeray then, as at other similar times, had no idea of giving pain, but when he saw a foible he put his foot upon it, and tried to stamp it out.

Such is my idea of the man whom many call a cynic, but whom I regard as one of the most soft-hearted of human beings, sweet as Charity itself, who went about the world dropping pearls, doing good, and never wilfully inflicting a wound.

CHAPTER II.

How Thackeray commenced his connection with *Fraser's Magazine* I am unable to say. We know how he had come to London with a view to a literary career, and that he had at one time made an attempt to earn his bread as a correspondent to a newspaper from Paris. It is probable that he became acquainted with the redoubtable Oliver Yorke, otherwise Dr. Maginn, or some of his staff, through the connection which he had thus opened with the press. He was not known, or at any rate he was unrecognized, by *Fraser* in January, 1835, in which month an amusing catalogue was given of the writers then employed, with portraits of them all seated at a symposium. I can trace no article to his pen before November, 1837, when the *Yellowplush Correspondence* was commenced, though it is hardly probable that he should have commenced with a work of so much pretension. There had been published a volume called *My Book, or the Anatomy of Conduct*, by John Skelton, and a very absurd book no doubt it was. We may presume that it contained maxims on etiquette, and that it was intended to convey in print those invaluable lessons on deportment which, as Dickens has told us, were subsequently given by Mr. Turveydrop, in the academy kept by him for that purpose. Thackeray took this as his foundation for the *Fashionable Fax and Polite Ax-ygoats*, by Jeames Yellowplush, with which he commenced those repeated attacks against snobbism which he delighted to make through a considerable portion of his literary life. Oliver Yorke has himself added four or five pages of his own to Thackeray's lucubrations; and with the second, and some future numbers, there appeared illustrations by Thackeray himself, illustrations at this time not having been common with the magazine. From all this I gather that the author was already held in estimation by *Fraser's* confraternity. I remember well my own delight with *Yellowplush* at the time, and how I inquired who was the author. It was then that I first heard Thackeray's name.

The *Yellowplush Papers* were continued through nine numbers. No further reference was made to Mr. Skelton and his book beyond that given at the beginning of the first number, and the satire is only shown by the attempt made by Yellowplush, the footman, to give his ideas generally on the manners of noble life. The idea seems to be that a gentleman may, in heart and in action, be as vulgar as a footman. No doubt he may, but the chances are very much that he won't. But the virtue of the memoir does not consist in the lessons, but in the general drollery of the letters. The "orthogwaphy is inaccuwate," as a certain person says in the memoirs—"so inaccuwate" as to take a positive study to "compwehend" it; but the joke, though old, is so handled as to be very amusing. Thackeray soon rushes away from his criticisms on snobbism to other matters. There are the details of a card-sharping enterprise, in which we cannot but feel that we recognise something of the author's own experiences in the misfortunes of Mr. Dawkins; there is the Earl of Crab's, and then

the first of those attacks which he was tempted to make
on the absurdities of his brethren of letters, and the only
one which now has the appearance of having been ill-nat-
ured. His first victims were Dr. Dionysius Lardner and
Mr. Edward Bulwer Lytton, as he was then. We can surrender the doctor to the whip of the satirist; and for
"Sawedwadgeorgeearllittnbulwig," as the novelist is made
to call himself, we can well believe that he must himself
have enjoyed the *Yellowplush Memoirs* if he ever re-read
them in after-life. The speech in which he is made to
dissuade the footman from joining the world of letters is
so good that I will venture to insert it: "Bullwig was vio-
lently affected; a tear stood in his glistening i. 'Yellowplush,' says he, seizing my hand, 'you *are* right. Quit
not your present occupation; black boots, clean knives,
wear plush all your life, but don't turn literary man. Look
at me. I am the first novelist in Europe. I have ranged
with eagle wings over the wide regions of literature, and
perched on every eminence in its turn. I have gazed with
eagle eyes on the sun of philosophy, and fathomed the
mysterious depths of the human mind. All languages are
familiar to me, all thoughts are known to me, all men understood by me. I have gathered wisdom from the hon-
eyed lips of Plato, as we wandered in the gardens of the
Academies; wisdom, too, from the mouth of Job Johnson,
as we smoked our backy in Seven Dials. Such must be
the studies, and such is the mission, in this world of the
Poet-Philosopher. But the knowledge is only emptiness;
the initiation is but misery ; the initiated a man shunned
and banned by his fellows. Oh!' said Bullwig, clasping
his hands, and throwing his fine i's up to the chandelier,
'the curse of Pwomethus descends upon his wace. Wath
and punishment pursue them from genewation to genewa-

tion! Wo to genius, the heaven-scaler, the fire-stealer! Wo and thrice-bitter desolation! Earth is the wock on which Zeus, wemorseless, stwetches his withing wictim;— men, the vultures that feed and fatten on him. Ai, ai! it is agony eternal—gwoaning and solitawy despair! And you, Yellowplush, would penetwate these mystewies; you would waise the awful veil, and stand in the twemendous Pwesence. Beware, as you value your peace, beware! Withdwaw, wash Neophyte! For heaven's sake! O for heaven's sake!'—Here he looked round with agony;—'give me a glass of bwandy-and-water, for this clawet is begin- ning to disagwee with me.' " It was thus that Thackeray began that vein of satire on his contemporaries of which it may be said that the older he grew the more amusing it was, and at the same time less likely to hurt the feelings of the author satirised.

The next tale of any length from Thackeray's pen, in the magazine, was that called *Catherine*, which is the story taken from the life of a wretched woman called Catherine Hayes. It is certainly not pleasant reading, and was not written with a pleasant purpose. It assumes to have come from the pen of Ikey Solomon, of Horse- monger Lane, and its object is to show how disgusting would be the records of thieves, cheats, and murderers if their doings and language were described according to their nature, instead of being handled in such a way as to create sympathy, and therefore imitation. Bulwer's *Eugene Aram*, Harrison Ainsworth's *Jack Sheppard*, and Dickens' Nancy were in his mind, and it was thus that he preached his sermon against the selection of such heroes and heroines by the novelists of the day. "Be it granted," he says, in his epilogue, "Solomon is dull; but don't attack his morality. He humbly submits that, in his poem, no man shall mistake virtue for vice, no man shall allow a single sentiment of pity or admiration to enter his bosom for any character in the poem, it being from beginning to end a scene of unmixed rascality, performed by persons who never deviate into good feeling." The intention is intelligible enough, but such a story neither could have been written nor read—certainly not written by Thackeray, nor read by the ordinary reader of a first-class magazine—had he not been enabled to adorn it by infinite wit. Captain Brock, though a brave man, is certainly not described as an interesting or gallant soldier; but he is possessed of great resources. Captain Macshane, too, is a thorough blackguard; but he is one with a dash of loyalty about him, so that the reader can almost sympathise with him, and is tempted to say that Ikey Solomon has not quite kept his promise.

Catherine appeared in 1839 and 1840. In the latter of those years *The Shabby Genteel* story also came out. Then, in 1841, there followed *The History of Samuel Titmarsh and the Great Hoggarty Diamond*, illustrated by Samuel's cousin, Michael Angelo. But though so announced in *Fraser*, there were no illustrations, and those attached to the story in later editions are not taken from sketches by Thackeray. This, as far as I know, was the first use of the name Titmarsh, and seems to indicate some intention on the part of the author of creating a hoax as to two personages—one the writer and the other the illustrator. If it were so, he must soon have dropped the idea. In the last paragraph he has shaken off his cousin Michael. The main object of the story is to expose the villany of bubble companies, and the danger they run who venture to have dealings with city matters which they do not understand. I cannot but think that he

4

altered his mind and changed his purpose while he was writing it, actuated probably by that editorial monition as to its length.

In 1842 were commenced *The Confessions of George Fitz-Boodle,* which were continued into 1843. I do not think that they attracted much attention, or that they have become peculiarly popular since. They are supposed to contain the reminiscences of a younger son, who moans over his poverty, complains of womankind generally, laughs at the world all round, and intersperses his pages with one or two excellent ballads. I quote one, written for the sake of affording a parody, with the parody along with it, because the two together give so strong an example of the condition of Thackeray's mind in regard to literary products. The "humbug" of everything, the pretence, the falseness of affected sentiment, the remoteness of poetical pathos from the true condition of the average minds of men and women, struck him so strongly, that he sometimes allowed himself almost to feel—or at any rate, to say—that poetical expression, as being above nature, must be unnatural. He had declared to himself that all humbug was odious, and should be by him laughed down to the extent of his capacity. His Yellowplush, his Catherine Hayes, his Fitz-Boodle, his Barry Lyndon, and Becky Sharp, with many others of this kind, were all invented and treated for this purpose and after this fashion. I shall have to say more on the same subject when I come to *The Snob Papers.* In this instance he wrote a very pretty ballad, *The Willow Tree*—so good that if left by itself it would create no idea of absurdity or extravagant pathos in the mind of the ordinary reader— simply that he might render his own work absurd by his own parody.

THE WILLOW-TREE.

No. I.

Know ye the willow-tree,
  Whose gray leaves quiver,
Whispering gloomily
  To yon pale river?
Lady, at eventide
  Wander not near it!
They say its branches hide
  A sad lost spirit!

Once to the willow-tree
  A maid came fearful,
Pale seemed her cheek to be,
  Her blue eye tearful.
Soon as she saw the tree,
  Her steps moved fleeter.
No one was there—ah me!—
  No one to meet her!

Quick beat her heart to hear
  The far bells' chime
Toll from the chapel-tower
  The trysting-time.
But the red sun went down
  In golden flame,
And though she looked around,
  Yet no one came!

Presently came the night,
  Sadly to greet her—
Moon in her silver light,
  Stars in their glitter.
Then sank the moon away
  Under the billow.
Still wept the maid alone—
  There by the willow!

THE WILLOW-TREE.

No. II.

Long by the willow-tree
  Vainly they sought her,
Wild rang the mother's screams
  O'er the gray water.
"Where is my lovely one?
  Where is my daughter?

Rouse thee, sir constable—
  Rouse thee and look.
Fisherman, bring your net,
  Boatman, your hook.
Beat in the lily-beds,
  Dive in the brook."

Vainly the constable
  Shouted and called her.
Vainly the fisherman
  Beat the green alder.
Vainly he threw the net.
  Never it hauled her!

Mother beside the fire
  Sat, her night-cap in;
Father in easy-chair,
  Gloomily napping;
When at the window-sill
  Came a light tapping.

And a pale countenance
  Looked through the casement.
Loud beat the mother's heart,
  Sick with amazement,
And at the vision which
  Came to surprise her!
Shrieking in an agony—
  "Lor'! it's Elizar!"

Through the long darkness,
  By the stream rolling,
Hour after hour went on
  Tolling and tolling.
Long was the darkness,
  Lonely and stilly.
Shrill came the night wind,
  Piercing and chilly.

Shrill blew the morning breeze,
  Biting and cold.
Bleak peers the gray dawn
  Over the wold!
Bleak over moor and stream
  Looks the gray dawn,
Gray with dishevelled hair.
  Still stands the willow there—
  The maid is gone!

Domine, Domine!
  Sing we a litany—
Sing for poor maiden-hearts
  broken and weary;
Sing we a litany,
Wail we and weep we a
  wild miserere!

Yes, 'twas Elizabeth;—
  Yes, 'twas their girl;
Pale was her cheek, and her
  Hair out of curl.
"Mother!" the loved one,
  Blushing exclaimed,
"Let not your innocent
  Lizzy be blamed.

Yesterday, going to Aunt
  Jones's to tea,
Mother, dear mother, I
  Forgot the door-key!
And as the night was cold,
  And the way steep,
Mrs. Jones kept me to
  Breakfast and sleep."

Whether her pa and ma
  Fully believed her,
That we shall never know.
  Stern they received her;
And for the work of that
  Cruel, though short, night—
Sent her to bed without
  Tea for a fortnight.

MORAL.

Hey diddle diddlety,
  Cat and the fiddlety,
Maidens of England take
  caution by she!
Let love and suicide
  Never tempt you aside,
And always remember to take
  the door-key!

Mr. George Fitz-Boodle gave his name to other narratives beyond his own *Confessions*. A series of stories was

carried on by him in *Fraser*, called *Men's Wives*, containing three : *Ravenwing*, *Mr. and Mrs. Frank Berry*, and
Dennis Hoggarty's Wife. The first chapter in *Mr. and
Mrs. Frank Berry* describes "The Fight at Slaughter
House." Slaughter House, as Mr. Venables reminded us
in the last chapter, was near Smithfield, in London—the
school which afterwards became Grey Friars; and the
fight between Biggs and Berry is the record of one which
took place in the flesh when Thackeray was at the Charter
House. But Mr. Fitz-Boodle's name was afterwards attached to a greater work than these, to a work so great
that subsequent editors have thought him to be unworthy
of the honour. In the January number, 1844, of *Fraser's
Magazine*, are commenced the *Memoirs of Barry Lyndon*,
and the authorship is attributed to Mr. Fitz-Boodle. The
title given in the magazine was *The Luck of Barry Lyndon : a Romance of the last Century*. By Fitz-Boodle.
In the collected edition of Thackeray's works the *Memoirs*
are given as "Written by himself," and were, I presume,
so brought out by Thackeray, after they had appeared in
Fraser. Why Mr. George Fitz-Boodle should have been
robbed of so great an honour I do not know.

In imagination, language, construction, and general literary capacity, Thackeray never did anything more remarkable than *Barry Lyndon*. I have quoted the words
which he put into the mouth of Ikey Solomon, declaring
that in the story which he has there told he has created
nothing but disgust for the wicked characters he has produced, and that he has "used his humble endeavours to
cause the public also to hate them." Here, in *Barry Lyndon*, he has, probably unconsciously, acted in direct opposition to his own principles. Barry Lyndon is as great a
scoundrel as the mind of man ever conceived. He is one

who might have taken as his motto Satan's words: "Evil, be thou my good." And yet his story is so written that it is almost impossible not to entertain something of a friendly feeling for him. He tells his own adventures as a card-sharper, bully, and liar; as a heartless wretch, who had neither love nor gratitude in his composition; who had no sense even of loyalty; who regarded gambling as the highest occupation to which a man could devote himself, and fraud as always justified by success; a man possessed by all meannesses except cowardice. And the reader is so carried away by his frankness and energy as almost to rejoice when he succeeds, and to grieve with him when he is brought to the ground.

The man is perfectly satisfied as to the reasonableness —I might almost say, as to the rectitude—of his own conduct throughout. He is one of a decayed Irish family, that could boast of good blood. His father had obtained possession of the remnants of the property by turning Protestant, thus ousting the elder brother, who later on becomes his nephew's confederate in gambling. The elder brother is true to the old religion, and as the law stood in the last century, the younger brother, by changing his religion, was able to turn him out. Barry, when a boy, learns the slang and the gait of the debauched gentlemen of the day. He is specially proud of being a gentleman by birth and manners. He had been kidnapped, and made to serve as a common soldier, but boasts that he was at once fit for the occasion when enabled to show as a court gentleman. "I came to it at once," he says, "and as if I had never done anything else all my life. I had a gentleman to wait upon me, a French *friseur* to dress my hair of a morning. I knew the taste of chocolate as by intuition almost, and could distinguish between the right Spanish

and the French before I had been a week in my new position. I had rings on all my fingers and watches in both
my fobs — canes, trinkets, and snuffboxes of all sorts. I
had the finest natural taste for lace and china of any man
I ever knew."

To dress well, to wear a sword with a grace, to carry
away his plunder with affected indifference, and to appear
to be equally easy when he loses his last ducat, to be
agreeable to women, and to look like a gentleman—these
are his accomplishments. In one place he rises to the
height of a grand professor in the art of gambling, and
gives his lessons with almost a noble air. "Play grandly,
honourably. Be not, of course, cast down at losing; but
above all, be not eager at winning, as mean souls are."
And he boasts of his accomplishments with so much eloquence as to make the reader sure that he believes in
them. He is quite pathetic over himself, and can describe
with heartrending words the evils that befall him when
others use against him successfully any of the arts which
he practises himself.

The marvel of the book is not so much that the hero
should evidently think well of himself, as that the author
should so tell his story as to appear to be altogether on
the hero's side. In *Catherine*, the horrors described are
most truly disgusting — so much that the story, though
very clever, is not pleasant reading. The *Memoirs of
Barry Lyndon* are very pleasant to read. There is nothing to shock or disgust. The style of narrative is exactly
that which might be used as to the exploits of a man
whom the author intended to represent as deserving of
sympathy and praise—so that the reader is almost brought
to sympathise. But I should be doing an injustice to
Thackeray if I were to leave an impression that he had

taught lessons tending to evil practice, such as he supposed to have been left by *Jack Sheppard* or *Eugene Aram*. No one will be tempted to undertake the life of a *chevalier d'industrie* by reading the book, or be made to think that cheating at cards is either an agreeable or a profitable profession. The following is excellent as a tirade in favour of gambling, coming from Redmond de Balibari, as he came to be called during his adventures abroad, but it will hardly persuade anyone to be a gambler:

"We always played on parole with anybody—any person, that is, of honour and noble lineage. We never pressed for our winnings, or declined to receive promissory notes in lieu of gold. But woe to the man who did not pay when the note became due! Redmond de Balibari was sure to wait upon him with his bill, and I promise you there were very few bad debts. On the contrary, gentlemen were grateful to us for our forbearance, and our character for honour stood unimpeached. In latter times, a vulgar national prejudice has chosen to cast a slur upon the character of men of honour engaged in the profession of play; but I speak of the good old days of Europe, before the cowardice of the French aristocracy (in the shameful revolution, which served them right) brought discredit upon our order. They cry fie now upon men engaged in play; but I should like to know how much more honourable *their* modes of livelihood are than ours. The broker of the Exchange, who bulls and bears, and buys and sells, and dabbles with lying loans, and trades upon state-secrets—what is he but a gamester? The merchant who deals in teas and tallow, is he any better? His bales of dirty indigo are his dice, his cards come up every year instead of every ten minutes, and the sea is his green-table. You call the profession of the law an honourable

one, where a man will lie for any bidder—lie down poverty for the sake of a fee from wealth; lie down right because wrong is in his brief.   You call a doctor an honourable man—a swindling quack who does not believe in the
nostrums which he prescribes, and takes your guinea for
whispering in your ear that it is a fine morning.   And
yet, forsooth, a gallant man, who sits him down before the
baize and challenges all comers, his money against theirs,
his fortune against theirs, is proscribed by your modern
moral world!   It is a conspiracy of the middle-class
against gentlemen.   It is only the shopkeeper cant which
is to go down nowadays.   I say that play was an institu-
tion of chivalry.   It has been wrecked along with other
privileges of men of birth.   When Seingalt engaged a
man for six-and-thirty hours without leaving the table, do
you think he showed no courage?   How have we had the
best blood, and the brightest eyes too, of Europe throbbing
round the table, as I and my uncle have held the cards
and the bank against some terrible player, who was match-
ing some thousands out of his millions against our all,
which was there on the baize!   When we engaged that
daring Alexis Kossloffsky, and won seven thousand louis
on a single coup, had we lost we should have been beggars
the next day; when *he* lost, he was only a village and a
few hundred serfs in pawn the worse.   When at Toeplitz
the Duke of Courland brought fourteen lacqueys, each
with four bags of florins, and challenged our bank to play
against the sealed bags, what did we ask?   'Sir,' said we,
'we have but eighty thousand florins in bank, or two hundred thousand at three months.   If your highness's bags
do not contain more than eighty thousand we will meet
you.'   And we did; and after eleven hours' play, in which
our bank was at one time reduced to two hundred and

4*

three ducats, we won seventeen thousand florins of him.
Is *this* not something like boldness? Does this profession
not require skill, and perseverance, and bravery? Four
crowned heads looked on at the game, and an imperial
princess, when I turned up the ace of hearts and made
Paroli, burst into tears. No man on the European Conti-
nent held a higher position than Redmond Barry then;
and when the Duke of Courland lost, he was pleased to
say that we had won nobly. And so we had, and spent
nobly what we won." This is very grand, and is put as
an eloquent man would put it who really wished to defend
gambling.

The rascal, of course, comes to a miserable end, but the
tone of the narrative is continued throughout. He is
brought to live at last with his old mother in the Fleet
prison, on a wretched annuity of fifty pounds per annum,
which she has saved out of the general wreck, and there
he dies of delirium tremens. For an assumed tone of continued irony, maintained through the long memoir of a
life, never becoming tedious, never unnatural, astounding
us rather by its naturalness, I know nothing equal to *Barry Lyndon.*

As one reads, one sometimes is struck by a conviction
that this or the other writer has thoroughly liked the work
on which he is engaged. There is a gusto about his
passages, a liveliness in the language, a spring in the mo-
tion of the words, an eagerness of description, a lilt, if I
may so call it, in the progress of the narrative, which
makes the reader feel that the author has himself greatly
enjoyed what he has written. He has evidently gone on
with his work without any sense of weariness or doubt;
and the words have come readily to him. So it has been
with *Barry Lyndon.* "My mind was filled full with those

blackguards," Thackeray once said to a friend. It is easy enough to see that it was so. In the passage which I have above quoted, his mind was running over with the idea that a rascal might be so far gone in rascality as to be in love with his own trade.

This was the last of Thackeray's long stories in *Fraser.* I have given by no means a complete catalogue of his contributions to the magazine, but I have perhaps mentioned those which are best known. There were many short pieces which have now been collected in his works, such as *Little Travels and Roadside Sketches*, and the *Carmen Lilliense*, in which the poet is supposed to be detained at Lille by want of money. There are others which I think are not to be found in the collected works, such as a *Box of Novels by Titmarsh*, and *Titmarsh in the Picture Galleries*. After the name of Titmarsh had been once assumed it was generally used in the papers which he sent to *Fraser.*

Thackeray's connection with *Punch* began in 1843, and, as far as I can learn, *Miss Tickletoby's Lectures on English History* was his first contribution. They, however, have not been found worthy of a place in the collected edition. His short pieces during a long period of his life were so numerous that to have brought them all together would have weighted his more important works with too great an amount of extraneous matter. The same lady, Miss Tickletoby, gave a series of lectures. There was *The History of the next French Revolution*, and *The Wanderings of our Fat Contributor* — the first of which is, and the latter is not, perpetuated in his works. Our old friend Jeames Yellowplush, or De la Pluche—for we cannot for a moment doubt that he is the same Jeames—is very prolific, and as excellent in his orthography, his sense, and

satire, as ever. These papers began with *The Lucky Spec-
ulator*. He lives in The Albany; he hires a brougham;
and is devoted to Miss Emily Flimsey, the daughter of Sir
George, who had been his master—to the great injury of
poor Maryanne, the fellow-servant who had loved him in
his kitchen days. Then there follows that wonderful ballad, *Jeames of Backley Square*. Upon this he writes an
angry letter to *Punch*, dated from his chambers in The
Albany: "Has a reglar suscriber to your amusing paper,
I beg leaf to state that I should never have done so had I
supposed that it was your 'abbit to igspose the mistaries
of privit life, and to hinger the delligit feelings of umble
individyouls like myself." He writes in his own defence,
both as to Maryanne and to the share-dealing by which he
had made his fortune; and he ends with declaring his
right to the position which he holds. "You are corrict
in stating that I am of hancient Normin fam'ly. This is
more than Peal can say, to whomb I applied for a bar-
netcy; but the primmier being of low igstraction, natrally
stikles for his horder." And the letter is signed "Fitzjames De la Pluche." Then follows his diary, beginning
with a description of the way in which he rushed into
Punch's office, declaring his misfortunes, when losses had
come upon him. "I wish to be paid for my contribew-
tions to your paper. Suckmstances is altered with me."
Whereupon he gets a cheque upon Messrs. Pump and Ald-
gate, and has himself carried away to new speculations.
He leaves his diary behind him, and *Punch* surreptitiously
publishes it. There is much in the diary which comes
from Thackeray's very heart. Who does not remember
his indignation against Lord Bareacres? "I gave the old
humbug a few shares out of my own pocket. 'There, old
Pride,' says I, 'I like to see you down on your knees to a

footman. There, old Pomposity! Take fifty pounds. I
like to see you come cringing and begging for it!' Whenever I see him in a very public place, I take my change
for my money. I digg him in the ribbs, or clap his padded old shoulders. I call him 'Bareacres, my old brick,'
and I see him wince. It does my 'art good." It does
Thackeray's heart good to pour himself out in indignation
against some imaginary Bareacres. He blows off his
steam with such an eagerness that he forgets for a time, or
nearly forgets, his cacography. Then there are "Jeames
on Time Bargings," "Jeames on the Guage Question,"
"Mr. Jeames again." Of all our author's heroes Jeames
is perhaps the most amusing. There is not much in that
joke of bad spelling, and we should have been inclined to
say beforehand, that Mrs. Malaprop had done it so well
and so sufficiently, that no repetition of it would be received with great favour. Like other dishes, it depends
upon the cooking. Jeames, with his "suckmstances," high
or low, will be immortal.

There were *The Travels in London*, a long series of
them; and then *Punch's Prize Novelists*, in which Thackeray imitates the language and plots of Bulwer, Disraeli,
Charles Lever, G. P. R. James, Mrs. Gore, and Cooper, the
American. They are all excellent; perhaps Codlingsby is
the best. Mendoza, when he is fighting with the barge-
man, or drinking with Codlingsby, or receiving Louis
Philippe in his rooms, seems to have come direct from
the pen of our Premier. Phil Fogerty's jump, and the
younger and the elder horsemen, as they come riding into
the story, one in his armour and the other with his feathers,
have the very savour and tone of Lever and James; but
then the savour and the tone are not so piquant. I know
nothing in the way of imitation to equal Codlingsby, if it

be not The Tale of Drury Lane, by W. S. in the *Rejected Addresses*, of which it is said that Walter Scott declared that he must have written it himself. The scene between Dr. Franklin, Louis XVI., Marie Antoinette, and Tatua, the chief of the Nose-rings, as told in *The Stars and Stripes*, is perfect in its way, but it fails as being a caricature of Cooper. The caricaturist has been carried away beyond and above his model, by his own sense of fun.

Of the ballads which appeared in *Punch* I will speak elsewhere, as I must give a separate short chapter to our author's power of versification; but I must say a word of *The Snob Papers*, which were at the time the most popular and the best known of all Thackeray's contributions to *Punch*. I think that perhaps they were more charming, more piquant, more apparently true, when they came out one after another in the periodical, than they are now as collected together. I think that one at a time would be better than many. And I think that the first half in the long list of snobs would have been more manifestly snobs to us than they are now with the second half of the list appended. In fact, there are too many of them, till the reader is driven to tell himself that the meaning of it all is that Adam's family is from first to last a family of snobs. "First," says Thackeray, in preface, "the world was made; then, as a matter of course, snobs; they existed for years and years, and were no more known than America. But presently—ingens patebat tellus—the people became darkly aware that there was such a race. Not above five-and-twenty years since, a name, an expressive monosyllable, arose to designate that case. That name has spread over England like railroads subsequently; snobs are known and recognised throughout an empire on which I am given to understand the sun never sets. *Punch* ap-

pears at the right season to chronicle their history; and
the individual comes forth to write that history in *Punch*.

"I have—and for this gift I congratulate myself with
a deep and abiding thankfulness—an eye for a snob. If
the truthful is the beautiful, it is beautiful to study even
the snobbish—to track snobs through history as certain
little dogs in Hampshire hunt out truffles; to sink shafts
in society, and come upon rich veins of snob-ore. Snobbishness is like Death, in a quotation from Horace, which
I hope you never heard, 'beating with equal foot at poor
men's doors, and kicking at the gates of emperors.' It is
a great mistake to judge of snobs lightly, and think they
exist among the lower classes merely. An immense per-
centage of snobs, I believe, is to be found in every rank of
this mortal life. You must not judge hastily or vulgarly
of snobs; to do so shows that you are yourself a snob. I
myself have been taken for one."

The state of Thackeray's mind when he commenced
his delineations of snobbery is here accurately depicted.
Written, as these papers were, for *Punch*, and written, as
they were, by Thackeray, it was a necessity that every
idea put forth should be given as a joke, and that the
satire on society in general should be wrapped up in burlesque absurdity. But not the less eager and serious was
his intention. When he tells us, at the end of the first
chapter, of a certain Colonel Snobley, whom he met at
"Bagnigge Wells," as he says, and with whom he was so
disgusted that he determined to drive the man out of the
house, we are well aware that he had met an offensive
military gentleman—probably at Tunbridge. Gentlemen
thus offensive, even though tamely offensive, were peculiarly offensive to him. We presume, by what follows, that
this gentleman, ignorantly—for himself most unfortunate-

ly—spoke of Publicōla. Thackeray was disgusted—disgusted that such a name should be lugged into ordinary
conversation at all, and then that a man should talk about
a name with which he was so little acquainted as not to
know how to pronounce it. The man was therefore a
snob, and ought to be put down; in all which I think that
Thackeray was unnecessarily hard on the man, and gave
him too much importance.

So it was with him in his whole intercourse with snobs
—as he calls them. He saw something that was distasteful, and a man instantly became a snob in his estimation.
"But you *can* draw," a man once said to him, there having been some discussion on the subject of Thackeray's
art powers. The man meant no doubt to be civil, but
meant also to imply that for the purpose needed the
drawing was good enough — a matter on which he was
competent to form an opinion. Thackeray instantly put
the man down as a snob for flattering him. The little
courtesies of the world and the little discourtesies became
snobbish to him. A man could not wear his hat, or carry
his umbrella, or mount his horse, without falling into some
error of snobbism before his hypercritical eyes. St. Michael would have carried his armour amiss, and St. Cecilia
have been snobbish as she twanged her harp.

I fancy that a policeman considers that every man in
the street would be properly " run in," if only all the truth
about the man had been known. The tinker thinks that
every pot is unsound. The cobbler doubts the stability
of every shoe. So at last it grew to be the case with
Thackeray. There was more hope that the city should
be saved because of its ten just men, than for society, if
society were to depend on ten who were not snobs. All
this arose from the keenness of his vision into that which

was really mean. But that keenness became so aggravated by the intenseness of his search that the slightest speck of dust became to his eyes as a foul stain. Publicōla, as we saw, damned one poor man to a wretched immortality, and another was called pitilessly over the coals because he had mixed a grain of flattery with a bushel of truth. Thackeray tells us that he was born to hunt out snobs, as certain dogs are trained to find truffles. But we can imagine that a dog, very energetic at producing truffles, and not finding them as plentiful as his heart desired, might occasionally produce roots which were not genuine—might be carried on in his energies till to his senses every fungus-root became a truffle. I think that there has been something of this with our author's snob-hunting, and that his zeal was at last greater than his discrimination.

The nature of the task which came upon him made this fault almost unavoidable. When a hit is made, say with a piece at a theatre, or with a set of illustrations, or with a series of papers on this or the other subject — when something of this kind has suited the taste of the moment, and gratified the public, there is a natural inclination on the part of those who are interested to continue that which has been found to be good. It pays and it pleases, and it seems to suit everybody. Then it is continued usque ad nauseam. We see it in everything. When the king said he liked partridges, partridges were served to him every day. The world was pleased with certain ridiculous portraits of its big men. The big men were soon used up, and the little men had to be added.

We can imagine that even *Punch* may occasionally be at a loss for subjects wherewith to delight its readers. In fact, *The Snob Papers* were too good to be brought to an end, and therefore there were forty-five of them. A dozen

would have been better. As he himself says in his last
paper, "for a mortal year we have been together flattering
and abusing the human race." It was exactly that. Of
course we know—everybody always knows—that a bad
specimen of his order may be found in every division of
society. There may be a snob king, a snob parson, a
snob member of parliament, a snob grocer, tailor, goldsmith, and the like. But that is not what has been meant.
We did not want a special satirist to tell us what we all
knew before. Had snobbishness been divided for us into
its various attributes and characteristics, rather than attributed to various classes, the end sought—the exposure,
namely, of the evil — would have been better attained.
The snobbishness of flattery, of falsehood, of cowardice,
lying, time-serving, money-worship, would have been perhaps attacked to a better purpose than that of kings,
priests, soldiers, merchants, or men of letters. The assault
as made by Thackeray seems to have been made on the
profession generally.

The paper on clerical snobs is intended to be essentially
generous, and is ended by an allusion to certain old clerical friends which has a sweet tone of tenderness in it.
"How should he who knows you, not respect you or your
calling? May this pen never write a pennyworth again if
it ever casts ridicule upon either." But in the mean time
he has thrown his stone at the covetousness of bishops,
because of certain Irish prelates who died rich many years
before he wrote. The insinuation is that bishops generally take more of the loaves and fishes than they ought,
whereas the fact is that bishops' incomes are generally so
insufficient for the requirements demanded of them, that
a feeling prevails that a clergyman to be fit for a bishop-
ric should have a private income. He attacks the snob-

bishness of the universities, showing us how one class of
young men consists of fellow-commoners, who wear lace
and drink wine with their meals, and another class consists of sizars, or servitors, who wear badges, as being poor,
and are never allowed to take their food with their fellow-
students. That arrangements fit for past times are not fit
for these is true enough. Consequently, they should gradually be changed, and from day to day are changed. But
there is no snobbishness in this. Was the fellow-com-
moner a snob when he acted in accordance with the custom of his rank and standing? or the sizar who accepted
aid in achieving that education which he could not have
got without it? or the tutor of the college, who carried
out the rules entrusted to him? There are two military
snobs, Rag and Famish. One is a swindler, and the other
a debauched young idiot. No doubt they are both snobs,
and one has been, while the other is, an officer. But there
is, I think, not an unfairness so much as an absence of
intuition, in attaching to soldiers especially two vices to
which all classes are open. Rag was a gambling snob, and
Famish a drunken snob; but they were not specially military snobs. There is a chapter devoted to dinner-giving
snobs, in which I think the doctrine laid down will not
hold water, and therefore that the snobbism imputed is
not proved. "Your usual style of meal," says the satirist
—"that is plenteous, comfortable, and in its perfection
—should be that to which you welcome your friends."
Then there is something said about the "Brummagem
plate pomp," and we are told that it is right that dukes
should give grand dinners, but that we—of the middle
class—should entertain our friends with the simplicity
which is customary with us. In all this there is, I think,
a mistake. The duke gives a grand dinner because he

thinks his friends will like it; sitting down when alone
with the duchess, we may suppose, with a retinue and
grandeur less than that which is arrayed for gala occasions. So is it with Mr. Jones, who is no snob because he
provides a costly dinner—if he can afford it. He does it
because he thinks his friends will like it. It may be that
the grand dinner is a bore—and that the leg of mutton,
with plenty of gravy and potatoes all hot, would be nicer.
I generally prefer the leg of mutton myself. But I do
not think that snobbery is involved in the other. A man,
no doubt, may be a snob in giving a dinner. I am not a
snob because for the occasion I eke out my own dozen
silver forks with plated ware; but if I make believe that
my plated ware is true silver, then I am a snob.

In that matter of association with our betters—we will
for the moment presume that gentlemen and ladies with
titles or great wealth are our betters—great and delicate
questions arise as to what is snobbery and what is not, in
speaking of which Thackeray becomes very indignant, and
explains the intensity of his feelings as thoroughly by a
charming little picture as by his words. It is a picture of
Queen Elizabeth as she is about to trample with disdain
on the coat which that snob Raleigh is throwing for her
use on the mud before her. This is intended to typify
the low parasite nature of the Englishman which has
been described in the previous page or two. "And of
these calm moralists"—it matters not for our present purpose who were the moralists in question—"is there one, I
wonder, whose heart would not throb with pleasure if he
could be seen walking arm-in-arm with a couple of dukes
down Pall Mall? No; it is impossible, in our condition
of society, not to be sometimes a snob." And again:
"How should it be otherwise in a country where lord-

olatry is part of our creed, and where our children are brought up to respect the 'Peerage' as the Englishman's second Bible?" Then follows the wonderfully graphic picture of Queen Elizabeth and Raleigh.

In all this Thackeray has been carried away from the truth by his hatred for a certain meanness of which there are no doubt examples enough. As for Raleigh, I think we have always sympathised with the young man, instead of despising him, because he felt on the impulse of the moment that nothing was too good for the woman and the queen combined. The idea of getting something in return for his coat could hardly have come so quick to him as that impulse in favour of royalty and womanhood. If one of us to-day should see the queen passing, would he not raise his hat, and assume, unconsciously, something of an altered demeanour because of his reverence for majesty? In doing so he would have no mean desire of getting anything. The throne and its occupant are to him honourable, and he honours them. There is surely no greater mistake than to suppose that reverence is snobbishness. I meet a great man in the street, and some chance having brought me to his knowledge, he stops and says a word to me. Am I a snob because I feel myself to be graced by his notice? Surely not. And if his acquaintance goes further and he asks me to dinner, am I not entitled so far to think well of myself because I have been found worthy of his society?

They who have raised themselves in the world, and they, too, whose position has enabled them to receive all that estimation can give, all that society can furnish, all that intercourse with the great can give, are more likely to be pleasant companions than they who have been less fortunate. That picture of two companion dukes in Pall

Mall is too gorgeous for human eye to endure. A man
would be scorched to cinders by so much light, as he
would be crushed by a sack of sovereigns even though he
might be allowed to have them if he could carry them
away. But there can be no doubt that a peer taken at
random as a companion would be preferable to a clerk
from a counting-house—taken at random. The clerk
might turn out a scholar on your hands, and the peer no
better than a poor spendthrift; but the chances are the
other way.

A tuft-hunter is a snob, a parasite is a snob, the man
who allows the manhood within him to be awed by a cor-
onet is a snob. The man who worships mere wealth is a
snob. But so also is he who, in fear lest he should be
called a snob, is afraid to seek the acquaintance—or if it
come to speak of the acquaintance—of those whose acquaintance is manifestly desirable. In all this I feel that
Thackeray was carried beyond the truth by his intense desire to put down what is mean.

It is in truth well for us all to know what constitutes
snobbism, and I think that Thackeray, had he not been
driven to dilution and dilatation, could have told us. If
you will keep your hands from picking and stealing, and
your tongue from evil speaking, lying, and slandering, you
will not be a snob. The lesson seems to be simple, and
perhaps a little trite, but if you look into it, it will be
found to contain nearly all that is necessary.

But the excellence of each individual picture as it is
drawn is not the less striking because there may be found
some fault with the series as a whole. What can excel
the telling of the story of Captain Shindy at his club—
which is, I must own, as true as it is graphic? Captain
Shindy is a real snob. "'Look at it, sir; is it cooked?

Smell it, sir. Is it meat fit for a gentleman?' he roars out
to the steward, who stands trembling before him, and who
in vain tells him that the Bishop of Bullocksmithy has
just had three from the same loin." The telling as re-
gards Captain Shindy is excellent, but the sidelong attack upon the episcopate is cruel. "All the waiters in the
club are huddled round the captain's mutton-chop. He
roars out the most horrible curses at John for not bringing the pickles. He utters the most dreadful oaths because Thomas has not arrived with the Harvey sauce.
Peter comes tumbling with the water-jug over Jeames,
who is bringing the 'glittering canisters with bread.'

   *   *   *   *   *   *   *

"Poor Mrs. Shindy and the children are, meanwhile, in
dingy lodgings somewhere, waited upon by a charity girl
in pattens."

The visit to Castle Carabas, and the housekeeper's description of the wonders of the family mansion, is as good.
"'The Side Entrance and 'All,' says the housekeeper.
'The halligator hover the mantelpiece was brought home
by Hadmiral St. Michaels, when a capting with Lord Han-
son. The harms on the cheers is the harms of the Carabas family. The great 'all is seventy feet in lenth, fifty-
six in breath, and thirty-eight feet 'igh. The carvings of
the chimlies, representing the buth of Venus and 'Ercules
and 'Eyelash, is by Van Chislum, the most famous sculpt-
ure of his hage and country. The ceiling, by Calimanco,
represents Painting, Harchitecture, and Music—the naked
female figure with the barrel-organ—introducing George,
first Lord Carabas, to the Temple of the Muses. The win-
der ornaments is by Vanderputty. The floor is Patago-
nian marble; and the chandelier in the centre was presented to Lionel, second marquis, by Lewy the Sixteenth,

whose 'ead was cut hoff in the French Revolution. We now henter the South Gallery," etc., etc. All of which is very good fun, with a dash of truth in it also as to the snobbery — only in this it will be necessary to be quite sure where the snobbery lies. If my Lord Carabas has a " buth of Venus," beautiful for all eyes to see, there is no snobbery, only good-nature, in the showing it ; nor is there snobbery in going to see it, if a beautiful " buth of Ve- nus" has charms for you. If you merely want to see the inside of a lord's house, and the lord is puffed up with the pride of showing his, then there will be two snobs.

Of all those papers it may be said that each has that quality of a pearl about it which in the previous chapter I endeavoured to explain. In each .some little point is made in excellent language, so as to charm by its neatness, incision, and drollery. But *The Snob Papers* had better be read separately, and not taken in the lump.

Thackeray ceased to write for *Punch* in 1852, either en· tirely or almost so.

CHAPTER III.

SOMETHING has been said, in the biographical chapter, of the way in which *Vanity Fair* was produced, and of the period in the author's life in which it was written. He had become famous—to a limited extent—by the exquisite nature of his contributions to periodicals; but he desired to do something larger, something greater, something, perhaps, less ephemeral. For though *Barry Lyndon* and others have not proved to be ephemeral, it was thus that he regarded them. In this spirit he went to work and wrote *Vanity Fair*.

It may be as well to speak first of the faults which were attributed to it. It was said that the good people were all fools, and that the clever people were all knaves. When the critics—the talking critics as well as the writing critics—began to discuss *Vanity Fair*, there had already grown up a feeling as to Thackeray as an author—that he was one who had taken up the business of castigating the vices of the world. Scott had dealt with the heroics, whether displayed in his Flora MacIvors or Meg Merrilieses, in his Ivanhoes or Ochiltrees. Miss Edgeworth had been moral; Miss Austen conventional; Bulwer had been poetical and sentimental; Marryatt and Lever had been funny and pugnacious, always with a dash of

5

gallantry, displaying funny naval and funny military life; and Dickens had already become great in painting the virtues of the lower orders. But by all these some kind of virtue had been sung, though it might be only the virtue of riding a horse or fighting a duel. Even Eugene Aram and Jack Sheppard, with whom Thackeray found so much fault, were intended to be fine fellows, though they broke into houses and committed murders. The primary object of all those writers was to create an interest by exciting sympathy. To enhance our sympathy personages were introduced who were very vile indeed—as Bucklaw, in the guise of a lover, to heighten our feelings for Ravenswood and Lucy; as Wild, as a thief-taker, to make us more anxious for the saving of Jack; as Ralph Nickleby, to pile up the pity for his niece Kate. But each of these novelists might have appropriately begun with an *Arma virumque cano*. The song was to be of something godlike—even with a Peter Simple. With Thackeray it had been altogether different. Alas, alas! the meanness of human wishes; the poorness of human results! That had been his tone. There can be no doubt that the heroic had appeared contemptible to him, as being untrue. The girl who had deceived her papa and mamma seemed more probable to him than she who perished under the willow-tree from sheer love—as given in the last chapter. Why sing songs that are false? Why tell of Lucy Ashtons and Kate Nicklebys, when pretty girls, let them be ever so beautiful, can be silly and sly? Why pour philosophy out of the mouth of a fashionable young gentleman like Pelham, seeing that young gentlemen of that sort rarely, or we may say never, talk after that fashion? Why make a house-breaker a gallant charming young fellow, the truth being that house-breakers as a rule are as objectionable in

their manners as they are in their morals? Thackeray's
mind had in truth worked in this way, and he had become
a satirist. That had been all very well for *Fraser* and
Punch; but when his satire was continued through a long
novel, in twenty-four parts, readers—who do in truth like
the heroic better than the wicked—began to declare that
this writer was no novelist, but only a cynic.

Thence the question arises what a novel should be—
which I will endeavour to discuss very shortly in a later
chapter. But this special fault was certainly found with
Vanity Fair at the time. Heroines should not only be
beautiful, but should be endowed also with a quasi celestial
grace—grace of dignity, propriety, and reticence. A heroine should hardly want to be married, the arrangement
being almost too mundane—and, should she be brought
to consent to undergo such bond, because of its acknowledged utility, it should be at some period so distant as
hardly to present itself to the mind as a reality. Eating
and drinking should be altogether indifferent to her, and
her clothes should be picturesque rather than smart, and
that from accident rather than design. Thackeray's
Amelia does not at all come up to the description here
given. She is proud of having a lover, constantly declaring to herself and to others that he is " the greatest and
the best of men "—whereas the young gentleman is, in
truth, a very little man. She is not at all indifferent as to
her finery, nor, as we see incidentally, to enjoying her sup-
pers at Vauxhall. She is anxious to be married—and as
soon as possible. A hero, too, should be dignified and of
a noble presence; a man who, though he may be as poor
as Nicholas Nickleby, should nevertheless be beautiful on
all occasions, and never deficient in readiness, address, or
self-assertion. *Vanity Fair* is specially declared by the

G   7

author to be "a novel without a hero," and therefore we
have hardly a right to complain of deficiency of heroic
conduct in any of the male characters.   But Captain Dobbin does become the hero, and is deficient.   Why was he
called Dobbin, except to make him ridiculous?   Why is
he so shamefully ugly, so shy, so awkward?   Why was he
the son of a grocer?   Thackeray in so depicting him was
determined to run counter to the recognised taste of novel
readers.   And then again there was the feeling of another
great fault.   Let there be the virtuous in a novel and let
there be the vicious, the dignified and the undignified, the
sublime and the ridiculous—only let the virtuous, the dignified, and the sublime be in the ascendant.   Edith Bellenden, and Lord Evandale, and Morton himself would be too
stilted, were they not enlivened by Mause, and Cuddie, and
Poundtext.   But here, in this novel, the vicious and the
absurd have been made to be of more importance than the
good and the noble.   Becky Sharp and Rawdon Crawley
are the real heroine and hero of the story.   It is with
them that the reader is called upon to interest himself.   It
is of them that he will think when he is reading the book.
It is by them that he will judge the book when he has
read it.   There was no doubt a feeling with the public
that though satire may be very well in its place, it should
not be made the backbone of a work so long and so important as this.   A short story such as *Catherine* or *Barry
Lyndon* might be pronounced to have been called for by
the iniquities of an outside world; but this seemed to
the readers to have been addressed almost to themselves.
Now men and women like to be painted as Titian would
paint them, or Raffaelle — not as Rembrandt, or even
Rubens.

Whether the ideal or the real is the best form of a

novel may be questioned, but there can be no doubt that
as there are novelists who cannot descend from the bright
heaven of the imagination to walk with their feet upon
the earth, so there are others to whom it is not given to
soar among clouds. The reader must please himself, and
make his selection if he cannot enjoy both. There are
many who are carried into a heaven of pathos by the woes
of a Master of Ravenswood, who fail altogether to be
touched by the enduring constancy of a Dobbin. There
are others—and I will not say but they may enjoy the
keenest delight which literature can give—who cannot
employ their minds on fiction unless it be conveyed in poetry. With Thackeray it was essential that the represen-
tations made by him should be, to his own thinking, life-
like. A Dobbin seemed to him to be such a one as might
probably be met with in the world, whereas to his thinking a Ravenswood was simply a creature of the imagination. He would have said of such, as we would say of
female faces by Raffaelle, that women would like to be
like them, but are not like them. Men might like to
be like Ravenswood, and women may dream of men so
formed and constituted, but such men do not exist. Dobbins do, and therefore Thackeray chose to write of a
Dobbin.

So also of the preference given to Becky Sharp and to
Rawdon Crawley. Thackeray thought that more can be
done by exposing the vices than extolling the virtues of
mankind. No doubt he had a more thorough belief in
the one than in the other. The Dobbins he did encoun-
ter—seldom ; the Rawdon Crawleys very often. He saw
around him so much that was mean ! He was hurt so
often by the little vanities of people ! It was thus that
he was driven to that overthoughtfulness about snobs of

which I have spoken in the last chapter. It thus became natural to him to insist on the thing which he hated with unceasing assiduity, and only to break out now and again into a rapture of love for the true nobility which was dear to him—as he did with the character of Captain Dobbin.

It must be added to all this, that, before he has done with his snob or his knave, he will generally weave in some little trait of humanity by which the sinner shall be relieved from the absolute darkness of utter iniquity. He deals with no Varneys or Deputy-Shepherds, all villany and all lies, because the snobs and knaves he had seen had never been all snob or all knave. Even Shindy probably had some feeling for the poor woman he left at home. Rawdon Crawley loved his wicked wife dearly, and there were moments even with her in which some redeeming trait half reconciles her to the reader.

Such were the faults which were found in *Vanity Fair;* but though the faults were found freely, the book was read by all. Those who are old enough can well remember the effect which it had, and the welcome which was given to the different numbers as they appeared. Though the story is vague and wandering, clearly commenced without any idea of an ending, yet there is something in the telling which makes every portion of it perfect in itself. There are absurdities in it which would not be admitted to anyone who had not a peculiar gift of making even his absurdities delightful. No school-girl who ever lived would have thrown back her gift-book, as Rebecca did the "dixonary," out of the carriage window as she was taken away from school. But who does not love that scene with which the novel commences? How could such a girl as Amelia Osborne have got herself into such society as that in which we see her at Vauxhall? But we forgive

it all because of the telling.   And then there is that crown-
ing absurdity of Sir Pitt Crawley and his establishment.

I never could understand how Thackeray in his first serious attempt could have dared to subject himself and Sir
Pitt Crawley to the critics of the time.   Sir Pitt is a baronet, a man of large property, and in Parliament, to whom
Becky Sharp goes as a governess at the end of a delightful
visit with her friend Amelia Sedley, on leaving Miss Pink-
erton's school.   The Sedley carriage takes her to Sir Pitt's
door.   " When the bell was rung a head appeared between
the interstices of the dining-room shutters, and the door
was opened by a man in drab breeches and gaiters, with a
dirty old coat, a foul old neckcloth lashed round his bris-
tly neck, a shining bald head, a leering red face, a pair
of twinkling gray eyes, and a mouth perpetually on the
grin.

" ' This Sir Pitt Crawley's ?' says John from the box.

" ' E'es,' says the man at the door, with a nod.

" ' Hand down these 'ere trunks there,' said John.

" ' Hand 'em down yourself,' said the porter."
But John on the box declines to do this, as he cannot
leave his horses.

" The bald - headed man, taking his hands out of his
breeches' pockets, advanced on this summons, and throwing Miss Sharp's trunk over his shoulder, carried it into
the house."   Then Becky is shown into the house, and a
dismantled dining-room is described, into which she is led
by the dirty man with the trunk.

Two kitchen chairs, and a round table, and an attenuated old poker
and tongs, were, however, gathered round the fireplace, as was a sauce-
pan over a feeble, sputtering fire.   There was a bit of cheese and
bread and a tin candlestick on the table, and a little black porter in
a pint pot.

"Had your dinner, I suppose?" This was said by him of the bald head. "It is not too warm for you? Like a drop of beer?"

"Where is Sir Pitt Crawley?" said Miss Sharp, majestically.

"He, he! *I*'m Sir Pitt Crawley. Rek'lect you owe me a pint for bringing down your luggage. He, he! ask Tinker if I ain't."

The lady addressed as Mrs. Tinker at this moment made her appearance, with a pipe and a paper of tobacco, for which she had been despatched a minute before Miss Sharp's arrival; and she handed the articles over to Sir Pitt, who had taken his seat by the fire.

"Where's the farden?" said he. "I gave you three half-pence; where's the change, old Tinker?"

"There," replied Mrs. Tinker, flinging down the coin. "It's only baronets as cares about farthings."

Sir Pitt Crawley has always been to me a stretch of audacity which I have been unable to understand. But it has been accepted; and from this commencement of Sir Pitt Crawley have grown the wonderful characters of the Crawley family — old Miss Crawley, the worldly, wicked, pleasure-loving aunt; the Rev. Bute Crawley and his wife, who are quite as worldly; the sanctimonious elder son, who in truth is not less so; and Rawdon, who ultimately becomes Becky's husband—who is the bad hero of the book, as Dobbin is the good hero. They are admirable; but it is quite clear that Thackeray had known nothing of what was coming about them when he caused Sir Pitt to eat his tripe with Mrs. Tinker in the London dining-room.

There is a double story running through the book, the parts of which are but lightly woven together, of which the former tells us the life and adventures of that singular young woman, Becky Sharp; and the other the troubles and ultimate success of our noble hero, Captain Dobbin. Though it be true that readers prefer, or pretend to prefer, the romantic to the common in their novels, and complain of pages which are defiled with that which is low, yet I find

that the absurd, the ludicrous, and even the evil, leave more
impression behind them than the grand, the beautiful, or
even the good.   Dominie Sampson, Dugald Dalgetty, and
Bothwell are, I think, more remembered than Fergus Mac-
Ivor, than Ivanhoe himself, or Mr. Butler the minister.   It
certainly came to pass that, in spite of the critics, Becky
Sharp became the first attraction in *Vanity Fair*.   When
we speak now of *Vanity Fair*, it is always to Becky that
our thoughts recur.   She has made a position for herself
in the world of fiction, and is one of our established personages.

  I have already said how she left school, throwing the
"dixonary" out of the window, like dust from her feet,
and was taken to spend a few halcyon weeks with her
friend Amelia Sedley, at the Sedley mansion in Russell
Square.   There she meets a brother Sedley home from India—the immortal Jos—at whom she began to set her
hitherto untried cap.   Here we become acquainted both
with the Sedley and with the Osborne families, with all
their domestic affections and domestic snobbery, and have
to confess that the snobbery is stronger than the affection.
As we desire to love Amelia Sedley, we wish that the people around her were less vulgar or less selfish—especially
we wish it in regard to that handsome young fellow, George
Osborne, whom she loves with her whole heart.   But with
Jos Sedley we are inclined to be content, though he be fat,
purse-proud, awkward, a drunkard, and a coward, because
we do not want anything better for Becky.   Becky does
not want anything better for herself, because the man has
money.   She has been born a pauper.   She knows herself
to be but ill qualified to set up as a beauty — though by
dint of cleverness she does succeed in that afterwards.
She has no advantages in regard to friends or family as

she enters life. She must earn her bread for herself.
Young as she is, she loves money, and has a great idea of
the power of money. Therefore, though Jos is distasteful
at all points, she instantly makes her attack. She fails,
however, at any rate for the present. She never becomes
his wife, but at last she succeeds in getting some of his
money. But before that time comes she has many a suffering to endure, and many a triumph to enjoy.

She goes to Sir Pitt Crawley as governess for his second family, and is taken down to Queen's Crawley in the
country. There her cleverness prevails, even with the
baronet, of whom I have just given Thackeray's portrait.
She keeps his accounts, and writes his letters, and helps
him to save money; she reads with the elder sister books
they ought not to have read; she flatters the sanctimonious son. In point of fact, she becomes all in all at Queen's
Crawley, so that Sir Pitt himself falls in love with her—
for there is reason to think that Sir Pitt may soon become again a widower. But there also came down to the
baronet's house, on an occasion of general entertaining,
Captain Rawdon Crawley. Of course Becky sets her cap
at him, and of course succeeds. She always succeeds.
Though she is only the governess, he insists upon dancing
with her, to the neglect of all the young ladies of the
neighbourhood. They continue to walk together by moon-
light—or starlight—the great, heavy, stupid, half-tipsy
dragoon, and the intriguing, covetous, altogether unprincipled young woman. And the two young people absolutely come to love one another in their way—the heavy,
stupid, fuddled dragoon, and the false, covetous, altogether
unprincipled young woman.

The fat aunt Crawley is a maiden lady, very rich, and
Becky quite succeeds in gaining the rich aunt by her

wiles. The aunt becomes so fond of Becky down in the country, that when she has to return to her own house in town, sick from over-eating, she cannot be happy without taking Becky with her. So Becky is installed in the house in London, having been taken away abruptly from her pupils, to the great dismay of the old lady's long-established resident companion. They all fall in love with her; she makes herself so charming, she is so clever; she can even, by help of a little care in dressing, become so picturesque! As all this goes on, the reader feels what a great personage is Miss Rebecca Sharp.

Lady Crawley dies down in the country, while Becky is still staying with his sister, who will not part with her. Sir Pitt at once rushes up to town, before the funeral, looking for consolation where only he can find it. Becky brings him down word from his sister's room that the old lady is too ill to see him.

"So much the better," Sir Pitt answered. "I want to see you, Miss Sharp. I want you back at Queen's Crawley, miss," the baronet said. His eyes had such a strange look, and were fixed upon her so stedfastly that Rebecca Sharp began almost to tremble. Then she half promises, talks about the dear children, and angles with the old man. "I tell you I want you," he says; "I'm going back to the vuneral, will you come back?—yes or no?"

"I daren't. I don't think—it wouldn't be right—to be alone—with you, sir," Becky said, seemingly in great agitation.

"I say again, I want you. I can't get on without you. I didn't see what it was till you went away. The house all goes wrong. It's not the same place. All my accounts has got muddled again. You must come back. Do come back. Dear Becky, do come."

"Come—as what, sir?" Rebecca gasped out.

"Come as Lady Crawley, if you like. There, will that zatisfy you? Come back and be my wife. You're vit for it. Birth be hanged. You're as good a lady as ever I see. You've got more brains in your little vinger than any baronet's wife in the country.

Will you come ? Yes or no ?" Rebecca is startled, but the old man goes on. " I'll make you happy; zee if I don't. You shall do what you like, spend what you like, and have it all your own way. I'll make you a settlement. I'll do everything regular. Look here," and the old man fell down on his knees and leered at her like a satyr.

But Rebecca, though she had been angling, angling for favour and love and power, had not expected this. For once in her life she loses her presence of mind, and exclaims : " Oh, Sir Pitt ; oh, sir ; I—I'm married already !" She has married Rawdon Crawley, Sir Pitt's younger son, Miss Crawley's favourite among those of her family who are looking for her money. But she keeps her secret for the present, and writes a charming letter to the Captain : " Dearest,—Something tells me that we shall conquer. You shall leave that odious regiment. Quit gaming, racing, and be a good boy, and we shall all live in Park Lane, and *ma tante* shall leave us all her money." *Ma tante's* money has been in her mind all through, but yet she loves him.

" Suppose the old lady doesn't come to," Rawdon said to his little wife as they sat together in the snug little Brompton lodgings. She had been trying the new piano all the morning. The new gloves fitted her to a nicety. The new shawl became her wonderfully. The new rings glittered on her little hands, and the new watch ticked at her waist.

" *I'll* make your fortune," she said ; and Delilah patted Samson's cheek.

" You can do anything," he said, kissing the little hand. " By Jove you can ! and we'll drive down to the Star and Garter and dine, by Jove !"

They were neither of them quite heartless at that moment, nor did Rawdon ever become quite bad. Then follow the adventures of Becky as a married woman, through

all of which there is a glimmer of love for her stupid husband, while it is the real purpose of her heart to get money
how she may—by her charms, by her wit, by her lies, by
her readiness. She makes love to everyone—even to her
sanctimonious brother-in-law, who becomes Sir Pitt in his
time—and always succeeds. But in her love-making there
is nothing of love. She gets hold of that well-remem-
bered old reprobate, the Marquis of Steyne, who possesses
the two valuable gifts of being very dissolute and very
rich, and from him she obtains money and jewels to her
heart's desire. The abominations of Lord Steyne are depicted in the strongest language of which *Vanity Fair*
admits. The reader's hair stands almost on end in horror at the wickedness of the two wretches—at her desire
for money, sheer money; and his for wickedness, sheer
wickedness. Then her husband finds her out—poor Rawdon! who with all his faults and thick-headed stupidity,
has become absolutely entranced by the wiles of his little
wife. He is carried off to a sponging-house, in order that
he may be out of the way, and, on escaping unexpectedly
from thraldom, finds the lord in his wife's drawing-room.
Whereupon he thrashes the old lord, nearly killing him;
takes away the plunder which he finds on his wife's person, and hurries away to seek assistance as to further re-
venge;—for he is determined to shoot the marquis, or to
be shot. He goes to one Captain Macmurdo, who is to
act as his second, and there he pours out his heart. "You
don't know how fond I was of that one," Rawdon said,
half-inarticulately. "Damme, I followed her like a footman! I gave up everything I had to her. I'm a beggar
because I would marry her. By Jove, sir, I've pawned my
own watch to get her anything she fancied. And she—
she's been making a purse for herself all the time, and

grudged me a hundred pounds to get me out of quod !"
His friend alleges that the wife may be innocent after all.
"It may be so," Rawdon exclaimed, sadly; "but this
don't look very innocent!" And he showed the captain
the thousand-pound note which he had found in Becky's
pocket-book.

But the marquis can do better than fight; and Rawdon, in spite of his true love, can do better than follow
the quarrel up to his own undoing. The marquis, on the
spur of the moment, gets the lady's husband appointed
governor of Coventry Island, with a salary of three thousand pounds a year; and poor Rawdon at last conde-
scends to accept the appointment. He will not see his
wife again, but he makes her an allowance out of his income.

In arranging all this, Thackeray is enabled to have a
side blow at the British way of distributing patronage—
for the favour of which he was afterwards himself a can-
didate. He quotes as follows from *The Royalist* newspaper : "We hear that the governorship "—of Coventry Isl-
and—" has been offered to Colonel Rawdon Crawley, C.B.,
a distinguished Waterloo officer. We need not only men
of acknowledged bravery, but men of administrative tal-
ents to superintend the affairs of our colonies; and we
have no doubt that the gentleman selected by the Colo-
nial Office to fill the lamented vacancy which has occurred
at Coventry Island is admirably calculated for the post."
The reader, however, is aware that the officer in question
cannot write a sentence or speak two words correctly.

Our heroine's adventures are carried on much further,
but they cannot be given here in detail. To the end she
is the same—utterly false, selfish, covetous, and successful.
To have made such a woman really in love would have

been a mistake. Her husband she likes best—because he
is, or was, her own. But there is no man so foul, so wicked, so unattractive, but that she can fawn over him for
money and jewels. There are women to whom nothing
is nasty, either in person, language, scenes, actions, or prin-
ciple—and Becky is one of them; and yet she is herself
attractive. A most wonderful sketch, for the perpetration
of which all Thackeray's power of combined indignation
and humour was necessary!

The story of Amelia and her two lovers, George Osborne
and Captain, or, as he came afterwards to be, Major, and
Colonel Dobbin, is less interesting, simply because goodness and eulogy are less exciting than wickedness and censure. Amelia is a true, honest-hearted, thoroughly English young woman, who loves her love because he is grand
—to her eyes—and loving him, loves him with all her
heart. Readers have said that she is silly, only because
she is not heroic. I do not know that she is more silly
than many young ladies whom we who are old have loved
in our youth, or than those whom our sons are loving at
the present time. Readers complain of Amelia because
she is absolutely true to nature. There are no Raffaellistic touches, no added graces, no divine romance. She is
feminine all over, and British—loving, true, thoroughly
unselfish, yet with a taste for having things comfortable,
forgiving, quite capable of jealousy, but prone to be ap-
peased at once, at the first kiss; quite convinced that her
lover, her husband, her children are the people in all the
world to whom the greatest consideration is due. Such
a one is sure to be the dupe of a Becky Sharp, should
a Becky Sharp come in her way—as is the case with so
many sweet Amelias whom we have known. But in a matter of love she is sound enough and sensible enough—and

she is as true as steel.   I know no trait in Amelia which
a man would be ashamed to find in his own daughter.

She marries her George Osborne, who, to tell the truth
of him, is but a poor kind of fellow, though he is a brave
soldier. He thinks much of his own person, and is selfish. Thackeray puts in a touch or two here and there by
which he is made to be odious.   He would rather give a
present to himself than to the girl who loved him.   Nevertheless, when her father is ruined he marries her, and he
fights bravely at Waterloo, and is killed.   "No more firing was heard at Brussels.   The pursuit rolled miles away.
Darkness came down on the field and the city ; and Amelia was praying for George, who was lying on his face,
dead, with a bullet through his heart."

Then follows the long courtship of Dobbin, the true
hero—he who has been the friend of George since their
old school-days ; who has lived with him and served him,
and has also loved Amelia.   But he has loved her—as
one man may love another—solely with a view to the
profit of his friend.   He has known all along that George
and Amelia have been engaged to each other as boy and
girl.   George would have neglected her, but Dobbin would
not allow it.   George would have jilted the girl who loved
him, but Dobbin would not let him.   He had nothing to
get for himself, but loving her as he did, it was the work
of his life to get for her all that she wanted.

George is shot at Waterloo, and then come fifteen
years of widowhood—fifteen years during which Becky
is carrying on her manœuvres—fifteen years during which
Amelia cannot bring herself to accept the devotion of the
old captain, who becomes at last a colonel.   But at the
end she is won.   "The vessel is in port.   He has got the
prize he has been trying for all his life.   The bird has

come in at last. There it is, with its head on its shoulder, billing and cooing clean up to his heart, with soft, out-stretched fluttering wings. This is what he has asked for every day and hour for eighteen years. This is what he has pined after. Here it is—the summit, the end, the last page of the third volume."

The reader as he closes the book has on his mind a strong conviction, the strongest possible conviction, that among men George is as weak and Dobbin as noble as any that he has met in literature; and that among women Amelia is as true and Becky as vile as any he has encoun-tered. Of so much he will be conscious. In addition to this he will unconsciously have found that every page he has read will have been of interest to him. There has been no padding, no longueurs; every bit will have had its weight with him. And he will find too at the end, if he will think of it—though readers, I fear, seldom think much of this in regard to books they have read—that the lesson taught in every page has been good. There may be details of evil painted so as to disgust—painted almost too plainly—but none painted so as to allure.

CHAPTER IV.

PENDENNIS AND THE NEWCOMES.

THE absence of the heroic was, in Thackeray, so palpable to Thackeray himself that in his original preface to *Pendennis*, when he began to be aware that his reputation was made, he tells his public what they may expect and what they may not, and makes his joking complaint of the readers of his time because they will not endure with patience the true picture of a natural man. " Even the gentlemen of our age," he says — adding that the story of *Pendennis* is an attempt to describe one of them, just as he is—" even those we cannot show as they are with the notorious selfishness of their time and their education. Since the author of *Tom Jones* was buried, no writer of fiction among us has been permitted to depict to his utmost power a MAN. We must shape him, and give him a certain conventional temper." Then he rebukes his audience because they will not listen to the truth. "You will not hear what moves in the real world, what passes in society, in the clubs, colleges, mess-rooms—what is the life and talk of your sons." You want the Raffaellistic touch, or that of some painter of horrors equally removed from the truth. I tell you how a man really does act— as did Fielding with Tom Jones—but it does not satisfy you. You will not sympathise with this young man of mine, this Pendennis, because he is neither angel nor imp. If it be so, let it be so. I will not paint for you angels or imps, because I do not see them. The young man of the day, whom I do see, and of whom I know the inside and the out thoroughly, him I have painted for you; and here he is, whether you like the picture or not.) This is what Thackeray meant, and, having this in his mind, he produced *Pendennis.*

(The object of a novel should be to instruct in morals while it amuses.) I cannot think but that every novelist who has thought much of his art will have realised as much as that for himself. Whether this may best be done by the transcendental or by the common-place is the question which it more behoves the reader than the author to answer, because the author may be fairly sure that he who can do the one will not, probably cannot, do the other. If a lad be only five feet high, he does not try to enlist in the Guards. Thackeray complains that many ladies have "remonstrated and subscribers left him," because of his realistic tendency. Nevertheless he has gone on with his work, and, in *Pendennis,* has painted a young man as natural as Tom Jones. Had he expended himself in the attempt, he could not have drawn a Master of Ravenswood.

It has to be admitted that Pendennis is not a fine fellow. He is not as weak, as selfish, as untrustworthy as that George Osborne whom Amelia married in *Vanity Fair;* but nevertheless, he is weak, and selfish, and untrustworthy.) He is not such a one as a father would wish to see his son, or a mother to welcome as a lover for her daughter. But then, fathers are so often doomed to find their sons not all that they wish, and mothers to see their girls falling in love with young men who are not

H   8

Paladins. In our individual lives we are contented to endure an admixture of evil, which we should resent if imputed to us in the general. We presume ourselves to be
truth-speaking, noble in our sentiments, generous in our
actions, modest and unselfish, chivalrous and devoted.
But we forgive and pass over in silence a few delinquencies among ourselves. What boy at school ever is a coward — in the general? What gentleman ever tells a lie?
What young lady is greedy? We take it for granted, as
though they were fixed rules in life, that our boys from
our public schools look us in the face and are manly; that
our gentlemen tell the truth as a matter of course; and
that our young ladies are refined and unselfish. Thackeray
is always protesting that it is not so, and that no good is
to be done by blinking the truth. He knows that we have
our little home experiences. Let us have the facts out, and
mend what is bad if we can. This novel of *Pendennis* is
one of his loudest protests to this effect.

I will not attempt to tell the story of Pendennis, how
his mother loved him, how he first came to be brought up
together with Laura Bell, how he thrashed the other boys
when he was a boy, and how he fell in love with Miss
Fotheringay, née Costigan, and was determined to marry
her while he was still a hobbledehoy, how he went up to
Boniface, that well-known college at Oxford, and there
did no good, spending money which he had not got, and
learning to gamble. The English gentleman, as we know,
never lies; but Pendennis is not quite truthful; when the
college tutor, thinking that he hears the rattling of dice,
makes his way into Pen's room, Pen and his two companions are found with three *Homers* before them, and Pen
asks the tutor with great gravity: "What was the present
condition of the river Scamander, and whether it was nav-

igable or no?" He tells his mother that, during a certain
vacation he must stay up and read, instead of coming
home—but, nevertheless, he goes up to London to amuse
himself. The reader is soon made to understand that,
though Pen may be a fine gentleman, he is not trust-
worthy. But he repents and comes home, and kisses his
mother; only, alas! he will always be kissing somebody
else also.

The story of the Amorys and the Claverings, and that
wonderful French cook M. Alcide Mirobolant, forms one
of those delightful digressions which Thackeray scatters
through his novels rather than weaves into them. They
generally have but little to do with the story itself, and
are brought in only as giving scope for some incident to
the real hero or heroine. But in this digression Pen is
very much concerned indeed, for he is brought to the
very verge of matrimony with that peculiarly disagreeable lady Miss Amory. He does escape at last, but only
within a few pages of the end, when we are made unhappy by the lady's victory over that poor young sinner
Foker, with whom we have all come to sympathise, in
spite of his vulgarity and fast propensities. She would
to the last fain have married Pen, in whom she believes,
thinking that he would make a name for her. "Il me
faut des émotions," says Blanche. Whereupon the author,
as he leaves her, explains the nature of this Miss Amory's
feelings. "For this young lady was not able to carry
out any emotion to the full, but had a sham enthusiasm,
a sham hatred, a sham love, a sham taste, a sham grief;
each of which flared and shone very vehemently for an
instant, but subsided and gave place to the next sham
emotion." Thackeray, when he drew this portrait, must
certainly have had some special young lady in his view.

But though we are made unhappy for Foker, Foker too escapes at last, and Blanche, with her emotions, marries that very doubtful nobleman Comte Montmorenci de Valentinois.

But all this of Miss Amory is but an episode. The purport of the story is the way in which the hero is made to enter upon the world, subject as he has been to the sweet teaching of his mother, and subject as he is made to be to the worldly lessons of his old uncle the major. Then he is ill, and nearly dies, and his mother comes up to nurse him. And there is his friend Warrington, of whose family down in Suffolk we shall have heard something when we have read *The Virginians*—one, I think, of the finest characters, as it is certainly one of the most touching, that Thackeray ever drew. Warrington, and Pen's mother, and Laura are our hero's better angels—angels so good as to make us wonder that a creature so weak should have had such angels about him; though we are driven to confess that their affection and loyalty for him are natural. There is a melancholy beneath the roughness of Warrington, and a feminine softness combined with the reticent manliness of the man, which have endeared him to readers beyond perhaps any character in the book. Major Pendennis has become immortal. Selfish, worldly, false, padded, caring altogether for things mean and poor in themselves; still the reader likes him. It is not quite all for himself. To Pen he is good—to Pen, who is the head of his family, and to come after him as the Pendennis of the day. To Pen and to Pen's mother he is beneficent after his lights. In whatever he undertakes, it is so contrived that the reader shall in some degree sympathise with him. And so it is with poor old Costigan, the drunken Irish captain, Miss

Fotheringay's papa. He was not a pleasant person. "We have witnessed the déshabille of Major Pendennis," says our author; " will any one wish to be valet-de-chambre to our other hero, Costigan? It would seem that the captain, before issuing from his bedroom, scented himself with otto of whisky." Yet there is a kindliness about him which softens our hearts, though in truth he is very careful that the kindness shall always be shown to himself.

Among these people Pen makes his way to the end of the novel, coming near to shipwreck on various occasions, and always deserving the shipwreck which he has almost encountered. Then there will arise the question whether it might not have been better that he should be altogether shipwrecked, rather than housed comfortably with such a wife as Laura, and left to that enjoyment of happiness forever after, which is the normal heaven prepared for heroes and heroines who have done their work well through three volumes. It is almost the only instance in all Thackeray's works in which this state of bliss is reached. George Osborne, who is the beautiful lover in *Vanity Fair*, is killed almost before our eyes, on the field of battle, and we feel that Nemesis has with justice taken hold of him. Poor old Dobbin does marry the widow, after fifteen years of further service, when we know him to be a middle-aged man and her a middle-aged woman. That glorious Paradise of which I have spoken requires a freshness which can hardly be attributed to the second marriage of a widow who has been fifteen years mourning for her first husband. Clive Newcome, "the first young man," if we may so call him, of the novel which I shall mention just now, is carried so far beyond his matrimonial elysium that we are allowed to see too plainly how far from true may be those promises of hymeneal happiness forever after. The cares of married life have settled down heavily upon his young head before we leave him. He not only marries, but loses his wife, and is left a melancholy widower with his son. Esmond and Beatrix certainly reach no such elysium as that of which we are speaking. But Pen, who surely deserved a Nemesis, though perhaps not one so black as that demanded by George Osborne's delinquencies, is treated as though he had been passed through the fire, and had come out—if not pure gold, still gold good enough for goldsmiths. "And what sort of a husband will this Pendennis be?" This is the question asked by the author himself at the end of the novel; feeling, no doubt, some hesitation as to the justice of what he had just done. "And what sort of a husband will this Pendennis be?" many a reader will ask, doubting the happiness of such a marriage and the future of Laura. The querists are referred to that lady herself, who, seeing his faults and wayward moods—seeing and owning that there are better men than he—loves him always with the most constant affection. The assertion could be made with perfect confidence, but is not to the purpose. That Laura's affection should be constant, no one would doubt; but more than that is wanted for happiness. How about Pendennis and his constancy?

The Newcomes, which I bracket in this chapter with *Pendennis*, was not written till after *Esmond*, and appeared between that novel and *The Virginians*, which was a sequel to *Esmond*. It is supposed to be edited by Pen, whose own adventures we have just completed, and is commenced by that celebrated night passed by Colonel Newcome and his boy Clive at the Cave of Harmony, during which the colonel is at first so pleasantly received and so genially entertained, but from which he is at last banished, indignant at the iniquities of our drunken old friend Captain Costigan, with whom we had become intimate in Pen's own memoirs. The boy Clive is described as being probably about sixteen. At the end of the story he has run through the adventures of his early life, and is left a melancholy man, a widower, one who has suffered the extremity of misery from a stepmother, and who is wrapped up in the only son that is left to him —as had been the case with his father at the beginning of the novel. (*The Newcomes*, therefore, like Thackeray's other tales, is rather a slice from the biographical memoirs of a family, than a romance or novel in itself.)

It is full of satire from the first to the last page. Every word of it seems to have been written to show how vile and poor a place this world is; how prone men are to deceive, how prone to be deceived. There is a scene in which "his Excellency Rummun Loll, otherwise his Highness Rummun Loll," is introduced to Colonel Newcome — or rather presented—for the two men had known each other before.   All London was talking of Rummun Loll, taking him for an Indian prince, but the colonel, who had served in India, knew better.   Rummun Loll was no more than a merchant, who had made a precarious fortune by doubtful means.   All the girls, nevertheless, are running after his Excellency.   "He's known to have two wives already in India," says Barnes Newcome; "but, by gad, for a settlement, I believe some of the girls here would marry him."   We have a delightful illustration of the London girls, with their bare necks and shoulders, sitting round Rummun Loll and worshipping him as he reposes on his low settee. There are a dozen of them so enchanted that the men who

wish to get a sight of the Rummun are quite kept at a
distance. This is satire on the women. A few pages on
we come upon a clergyman who is no more real than Rummun Loll. The clergyman, Charles Honeyman, had married the colonel's sister and had lost his wife, and now the
brothers-in-law meet. "'Poor, poor Emma!' exclaimed
the ecclesiastic, casting his eyes towards the chandelier and
passing a white cambric pocket-handkerchief gracefully
before them. No man in London understood the ring
business or the pocket-handkerchief business better, or
smothered his emotion more beautifully. 'In the gayest
moments, in the giddiest throng of fashion, the thoughts
of the past will rise; the departed will be among us still.
But this is not the strain wherewith to greet the friend
newly arrived on our shores. How it rejoices me to behold you in old England!'" And so the satirist goes on
with Mr. Honeyman the clergyman. Mr. Honeyman the
clergyman has been already mentioned, in that extract
made in our first chapter from *Lovel the Widower*. It
was he who assisted another friend, "with his wheedling
tongue," in inducing Thackeray to purchase that "neat
little literary paper"—called then *The Museum*, but which
was in truth *The National Standard*. In describing
Barnes Newcome, the colonel's relative, Thackeray in the
same scene attacks the sharpness of the young men of business of the present day. There were, or were to be, some
transactions with Rummun Loll, and Barnes Newcome, being in doubt, asks the colonel a question or two as to the
certainty of the Rummun's money, much to the colonel's
disgust. "The young man of business had dropped his
drawl or his languor, and was speaking quite unaffectedly,
good-naturedly, and selfishly. Had you talked to him for
a week you would not have made him understand the

scorn and loathing with which the colonel regarded him. Here was a young fellow as keen as the oldest curmudgeon—a lad with scarce a beard to his chin, that would pursue his bond as rigidly as Shylock." "Barnes Newcome never missed a church," he goes on, " or dressing for dinner. He never kept a tradesman waiting for his money. He seldom drank too much, and never was late for business, or huddled over his toilet, however brief his sleep or severe his headache. In a word, he was as scrupulously whited as any sepulchre in the whole bills of mortality." Thackeray had lately seen some Barnes Newcome when he wrote that.

It is all satire; but there is generally a touch of pathos even through the satire. It is satire when Miss Quigley, the governess in Park Street, falls in love with the old colonel after some dim fashion of her own. "When she is walking with her little charges in the Park, faint signals of welcome appear on her wan cheeks. She knows the dear colonel amidst a thousand horsemen." The colonel had drunk a glass of wine with her after his stately fashion, and the foolish old maid thinks too much of it. Then we are told how she knits purses for him, " as she sits alone in the schoolroom — high up in that lone house, when the little ones are long since asleep—before her dismal little tea-tray, and her little desk containing her mother's letters and her mementoes of home." Miss Quigley is an ass; but we are made to sympathise entirely with the ass, because of that morsel of pathos as to her mother's letters.

Clive Newcome, our hero, who is a second Pen, but a better fellow, is himself a satire on young men—on young men who are idle and ambitious at the same time. He is a painter ; but, instead of being proud of his art, is half ashamed of it—because not being industrious he has not, while yet young, learned to excel. He is "doing" a portrait of Mrs. Pendennis, Laura, and thus speaks of his business. "No. 666"—he is supposed to be quoting from the catalogue of the Royal Academy for the year—"No. 666. Portrait of Joseph Muggins, Esq., Newcome, George Street. No. 979. Portrait of Mrs. Muggins on her gray pony, Newcome. No. 579. Portrait of Joseph Muggins, Esq.'s dog Toby, Newcome. This is what I am fit for. These are the victories I have set myself on achieving. Oh, Mrs. Pendennis! isn't it humiliating? Why isn't there a war? Why haven't I a genius? There is a painter who lives hard by, and who begs me to come and look at his work. He is in the Muggins line too. He gets his canvases with a good light upon them; excludes the contemplation of other objects; stands beside his picture in an attitude himself; and thinks that he and they are masterpieces. Oh me, what drivelling wretches we are! Fame! — except that of just the one or two—what's the use of it?" In all of which Thackeray is speaking his own feelings about himself as well as the world at large. What's the use of it all? Oh vanitas vanitatum! Oh vanity and vexation of spirit! "So Clive Newcome," he says afterwards, "lay on a bed of down and tossed and tumbled there. He went to fine dinners, and sat silent over them; rode fine horses, and black care jumped up behind the moody horseman." As I write this I have before me a letter from Thackeray to a friend describing his own success when *Vanity Fair* was coming out, full of the same feeling. He is making money, but he spends it so fast that he never has any; and as for the opinions expressed on his books, he cares little for what he hears. There was always present to him a feeling of black care seated be-

hind the horseman—and would have been equally so had
there been no real care present to him. A sardonic melancholy was the characteristic most common to him—
which, however, was relieved by an always present capacity for instant frolic. It was these attributes combined
which made him of all satirists the most humorous, and of
all humorists the most satirical. It was these that produced the Osbornes, the Dobbins, the Pens, the Clives, and
the Newcomes, whom, when he loved them the most, he
could not save himself from describing as mean and unworthy. A somewhat heroic hero of romance—such a
one, let us say, as Waverley, or Lovel in *The Antiquary*, or
Morton in *Old Mortality*—was revolting to him, as lacking those foibles which human nature seemed to him to
demand.

The story ends with two sad tragedies, neither of which
would have been demanded by the story, had not such
sadness been agreeable to the author's own idiosyncrasy.
The one is the ruin of the old colonel's fortunes, he having allowed himself to be enticed into bubble speculations;
and the other is the loss of all happiness, and even comfort, to Clive the hero, by the abominations of his mother-
in-law. The woman is so iniquitous, and so tremendous
in her iniquities, that she rises to tragedy. Who does not
know Mrs. Mack the Campaigner? Why at the end of his
long story should Thackeray have married his hero to so
lackadaisical a heroine as poor little Rosey, or brought on
the stage such a she-demon as Rosey's mother? But there
is the Campaigner in all her vigour, a marvel of strength
of composition—one of the most vividly drawn characters
in fiction—but a woman so odious that one is induced to
doubt whether she should have been depicted.

The other tragedy is altogether of a different kind, and

though unnecessary to the story, and contrary to that practice of story-telling which seems to demand that calamities to those personages with whom we are to sympathise should not be brought in at the close of a work of fiction, is so beautifully told that no lover of Thackeray's work would be willing to part with it. The old colonel, as we have said, is ruined by speculation, and in his ruin is brought to accept the alms of the brotherhood of the Grey Friars. Then we are introduced to the Charter House, at which, as most of us know, there still exists a brotherhood of the kind. He dons the gown — this old colonel, who had always been comfortable in his means, and latterly apparently rich — and occupies the single room, and eats the doled bread, and among his poor brothers sits in the chapel of his order. The description is perhaps as fine as anything that Thackeray ever did. The gentleman is still the gentleman, with all the pride of gentry ;—but not the less is he the humble bedesman, aware that he is living upon charity, not made to grovel by any sense of shame, but knowing that, though his normal pride may be left to him, an outward demeanour of humility is befitting.

And then he dies. "At the usual evening hour the chapel bell began to toll, and Thomas Newcome's hands outside the bed feebly beat time—and just as the last bell struck, a peculiar sweet smile shone over his face, and he lifted up his head a little, and quickly said, 'Adsum'—and fell back. It was the word we used at school when names were called ; and, lo, he whose heart was as that of a little child had answered to his name, and stood in the presence of his Maker !"

CHAPTER V.

ESMOND AND THE VIRGINIANS.

THE novel with which we are now going to deal I regard
as the greatest work that Thackeray did. Though I do
not hesitate to compare himself with himself, I will make
no comparison between him and others; I therefore ab-
stain from assigning to *Esmond* any special niche among
prose fictions in the English language, but I rank it so
high as to justify me in placing him among the small
number of the highest class of English novelists. Much as
I think of *Barry Lyndon* and *Vanity Fair*, I cannot quite
say this of them; but, as a chain is not stronger than its
weakest link, so is a poet, or a dramatist, or a novelist to
be placed in no lower level than that which he has attained
by his highest sustained flight. The excellence which has
been reached here Thackeray achieved, without doubt, by
giving a greater amount of forethought to the work he
had before him than had been his wont. When we were
young we used to be told, in our house at home, that " elbow-grease " was the one essential necessary to getting a
tough piece of work well done. If a mahogany table was
to be made to shine, it was elbow-grease that the operation
needed. Forethought is the elbow-grease which a novelist
—or poet—or dramatist—requires. It is not only his plot
that has to be turned and re-turned in his mind, not his

plot chiefly, but he has to make himself sure of his situations, of his characters, of his effects, so that when the time comes for hitting the nail he may know where to hit it on the head—so that he may himself understand the passion, the calmness, the virtues, the vices, the rewards and punishments which he means to explain to others—so that his proportions shall be correct, and he be saved from the absurdity of devoting two-thirds of his book to the beginning, or two-thirds to the completion of his task. It is from want of this special labour, more frequently than from intellectual deficiency, that the tellers of stories fail so often to hit their nails on the head. To think of a story is much harder work than to write it. The author can sit down with the pen in his hand for a given time, and produce a certain number of words. That is comparatively easy, and if he have a conscience in regard to his task, work will be done regularly. But to think it over as you lie in bed, or walk about, or sit cosily over your fire, to turn it all in your thoughts, and make the things fit—that requires elbow-grease of the mind. The arrangement of the words is as though you were walking simply along a road. The arrangement of your story is as though you were carrying a sack of flour while you walked. Fielding had carried his sack of flour before he wrote *Tom Jones,* and Scott his before he produced *Ivanhoe.* So had Thackeray done—a very heavy sack of flour—in creating *Esmond.* In *Vanity Fair,* in *Pendennis,* and in *The New-comes,* there was more of that mere wandering in which no heavy burden was borne. The richness of the author's mind, the beauty of his language, his imagination and perception of character, are all there. For that which was lovely he has shown his love, and for the hateful his hatred; but, nevertheless, they are comparatively idle books. His only work, as far as I can judge them, in which there is no touch of idleness, is *Esmond*. *Barry Lyndon* is consecutive, and has the well-sustained purpose of exhibiting a finished rascal; but *Barry Lyndon* is not quite the same from beginning to end. All his full-fledged novels, except *Esmond*, contain rather strings of incidents and memoirs of individuals, than a completed story. But *Esmond* is a whole from beginning to end, with its tale well told, its purpose developed, its moral brought home— and its nail hit well on the head and driven in.

I told Thackeray once that it was not only his best work, but so much the best, that there was none second to it. "That was what I intended," he said, "but I have failed. Nobody reads it. After all, what does it matter?" he went on after awhile. "If they like anything, one ought to be satisfied. After all, Esmond was a prig." Then he laughed and changed the subject, not caring to dwell on thoughts painful to him. The elbow-grease of thinking was always distasteful to him, and had no doubt been so when he conceived and carried out this work.

To the ordinary labour necessary for such a novel he added very much by his resolution to write it in a style different, not only from that which he had made his own, but from that also which belonged to the time. He had devoted himself to the reading of the literature of Queen Anne's reign, and having chosen to throw his story into that period, and to create in it personages who were to be peculiarly concerned with the period, he resolved to use as the vehicle for his story the forms of expression then prevalent. No one who has not tried it can understand how great is the difficulty of mastering a phase of one's own language other than that which habit has made familiar. To write in another language, if the language be suffi-

6*

ciently known, is a much less arduous undertaking. The
lad who attempts to write his essay in Ciceronian Latin
struggles to achieve a style which is not indeed common
to him, but is more common than any other he has become acquainted with in that tongue. But Thackeray in
his work had always to remember his Swift, his Steele,
and his Addison, and to forget at the same time the modes
of expression which the day had adopted. Whether he
asked advice on the subject, I do not know. But I feel
sure that if he did he must have been counselled against
it. Let my reader think what advice he would give to
any writer on such a subject. Probably he asked no advice, and would have taken none. No doubt he found
himself, at first imperceptibly, gliding into a phraseology
which had attractions for his ear, and then probably was
so charmed with the peculiarly masculine forms of sentences which thus became familiar to him, that he thought
it would be almost as difficult to drop them altogether as
altogether to assume the use of them. And if he could do
so successfully, how great would be the assistance given
to the local colouring which is needed for a novel in prose,
the scene of which is thrown far back from the writer's
period! Were I to write a poem about Cœur de Lion, I
should not mar my poem by using the simple language of
the day; but if I write a prose story of the time, I cannot
altogether avoid some attempt at far-away quaintnesses in
language. To call a purse a " gypsire," and to begin your
little speeches with " Marry come up," or to finish them
with " Quotha," are but poor attempts. But even they
have had their effect. Scott did the best he could with
his Cœur de Lion. When we look to it we find that it
was but little; though in his hands it passed for much.
" By my troth," said the knight, " thou hast sung well and

heartily, and in high praise of thine order." We doubt
whether he achieved any similarity to the language of the
time; but still, even in the little which he attempted, there
was something of the picturesque.   But how much more
would be done if in very truth the whole language of a
story could be thrown with correctness into the form of
expression used at the time depicted?

It was this that Thackeray tried in his *Esmond*, and he
has done it almost without a flaw.   The time in question
is near enough to us, and the literature sufficiently familiar
to enable us to judge.   Whether folk swore by their troth
in the days of King Richard I. we do not know, but when
we read Swift's letters, and Addison's papers, or Defoe's
novels, we do catch the veritable sounds of Queen Anne's
age, and can say for ourselves whether Thackeray has
caught them correctly or not.   No reader can doubt that
he has done so.   Nor is the reader ever struck with the
affectation of an assumed dialect.   The words come as
though they had been written naturally—though not natural to the middle of the nineteenth century.   It was a
tour de force, and successful as such a *tour de force* so
seldom is.   But though Thackeray was successful in adopt-
ing the tone he wished to assume, he never quite succeeded, as far as my ear can judge, in altogether dropping it
again.

And yet it has to be remembered that though *Esmond*
deals with the times of Queen Anne, and "copies the language" of the time, as Thackeray himself says in the dedication, the story is not supposed to have been written till
the reign of George II.   Esmond in his narrative speaks
of Fielding and Hogarth, who did their best work under
George II.   The idea is that Henry Esmond, the hero,
went out to Virginia after the events told, and there wrote

I   9

the memoir in the form of an autobiography. The estate of Castlewood, in Virginia, had been given to the Esmond family by Charles II.; and this Esmond, our hero, finding that expatriation would best suit both his domestic happiness and his political difficulties—as the reader of the book will understand might be the case—settles himself in the colony, and there writes the history of his early life. He retains the manners, and with the manners the language of his youth. He lives among his own people, a country gentleman with a broad domain, mixing but little with the world beyond, and remains an English gentleman of the time of Queen Anne. The story is continued in *The Virginians*, the name given to a record of two lads who were grandsons of Harry Esmond, whose names are Warrington. Before *The Virginians* appeared we had already become acquainted with a scion of that family, the friend of Arthur Pendennis, a younger son of Sir Miles Warrington, of Suffolk. Henry Esmond's daughter had in a previous generation married a younger son of the then baronet. This is mentioned now to show the way in which Thackeray's mind worked afterwards upon the details and characters which he had originated in *Esmond*.

It is not my purpose to tell the story here, but rather to explain the way in which it is written, to show how it differs from other stories, and thus to explain its effect. Harry Esmond, who tells the story, is of course the hero. There are two heroines who equally command our sympathy—Lady Castlewood, the wife of Harry's kinsman, and her daughter Beatrix. Thackeray himself declared the man to be a prig, and he was not altogether wrong. Beatrix, with whom throughout the whole book he is in love, knew him well. "Shall I be frank with you, Harry," she says, when she is engaged to another suitor, "and say that if you had not been down on your knees and so humble, you might have fared better with me? A woman of my spirit, cousin, is to be won by gallantry, and not by sighs and rueful faces. All the time you are worshipping and singing hymns to me, I know very well I am no goddess." And again: "As for you, you want a woman to bring your slippers and cap, and to sit at your feet and cry, O caro, caro! O bravo! whilst you read your Shakespeares and Miltons and stuff." He was a prig, and the girl he loved knew him, and being quite of another way of thinking herself, would have nothing to say to him in the way of love. But without something of the aptitudes of a prig the character which the author intended could not have been drawn. There was to be courage — military courage—and that propensity to fighting which the tone of the age demanded in a finished gentleman. Esmond, therefore, is ready enough to use his sword. But at the same time he has to live as becomes one whose name is in some degree under a cloud; for though he be not in truth an illegitimate offshoot of the noble family which is his, and though he knows that he is not so, still he has to live as though he were. He becomes a soldier, and it was just then that our army was accustomed "to swear horribly in Flanders." But Esmond likes his books, and cannot swear or drink like other soldiers. Nevertheless he has a sort of liking for fast ways in others, knowing that such are the ways of a gallant cavalier. There is a melancholy over his life which makes him always, to himself and to others, much older than his years. He is well aware that, being as he is, it is impossible that Beatrix should love him. Now and then there is a dash of lightness about him, as though he had taught himself, in his philosophy, that even sorrow may be borne with a smile—as though

there was something in him of the Stoic's doctrine, which
made him feel that even disappointed love should not be
seen to wound too deep. But still, when he smiles, even
when he indulges in some little pleasantry, there is that
garb of melancholy over him which always makes a man a
prig. But he is a gentleman from the crown of his head
to the sole of his foot. Thackeray had let the whole
power of his intellect apply itself to a conception of the
character of a gentleman. This man is brave, polished,
gifted with that old-fashioned courtesy which ladies used
to love, true as steel, loyal as faith himself, with a power
of self-abnegation which astonishes the criticising reader
when he finds such a virtue carried to such an extent without seeming to be unnatural. To draw the picture of a
man, and say that he is gifted with all the virtues, is easy
enough—easy enough to describe him as performing all
the virtues. The difficulty is to put your man on his legs,
and make him move about, carrying his virtues with a natural gait, so that the reader shall feel that he is becoming
acquainted with flesh and blood, not with a wooden figure.
The virtues are all there with Henry Esmond, and the
flesh and blood also, so that the reader believes in them.
But still there is left a flavour of the character which
Thackeray himself tasted when he called his hero a prig.

The two heroines, Lady Castlewood and Beatrix, are
mother and daughter, of whom the former is in love with
Esmond, and the latter is loved by him. Fault has been
found with the story, because of the unnatural rivalry—
because it has been felt that a mother's solicitude for her
daughter should admit of no such juxtaposition. But the
criticism has come, I think, from those who have failed to
understand, not from those who have understood the tale;
not because they have read it, but because they have not

read it, and have only looked at it or heard of it. Lady
Castlewood is perhaps ten years older than the boy Esmond, whom she first finds in her husband's house, and
takes as a *protégé;* and from the moment in which she
finds that he is in love with her own daughter, she does
her best to bring about a marriage between them. Her
husband is alive, and though he is a drunken brute—after
the manner of lords of that time—she is thoroughly loyal
to him. The little touches, of which the woman is herself
altogether unconscious, that gradually turn a love for the
boy into a love for the man, are told so delicately, that it
is only at last that the reader perceives what has in truth
happened to the woman. She is angry with him, grateful to him, careful over him, gradually conscious of all his
worth, and of all that he does to her and hers, till at last
her heart is unable to resist. But then she is a widow;—
and Beatrix has declared that her ambition will not allow
her to marry so humble a swain, and Esmond has become
—as he says of himself when he calls himself " an old gentleman "—" the guardian of all the family," "fit to be the
grandfather of you all."

The character of Lady Castlewood has required more
delicacy in its manipulation than perhaps any other which
Thackeray has drawn. There is a mixture in it of self-
negation and of jealousy, of gratefulness of heart and of
the weary thoughtfulness of age, of occasional sprightli-
ness with deep melancholy, of injustice with a thorough
appreciation of the good around her, of personal weakness
—as shown always in her intercourse with her children,
and of personal strength — as displayed when she vindi-
cates the position of her kinsman Henry to the Duke of
Hamilton, who is about to marry Beatrix;—a mixture
which has required a master's hand to trace. These con-

tradictions are essentially feminine. Perhaps it must be
confessed that in the unreasonableness of the woman, the
author has intended to bear more harshly on the sex than
it deserves. But a true woman will forgive him, because
of the truth of Lady Castlewood's heart. Her husband
had been killed in a duel, and there were circumstances
which had induced her at the moment to quarrel with
Harry and to be unjust to him. He had been ill, and
had gone away to the wars, and then she had learned the
truth, and had been wretched enough. But when he
comes back, and she sees him, by chance at first, as the
anthem is being sung in the cathedral choir, as she is saying her prayers, her heart flows over with tenderness to
him. "I knew you would come back," she said; "and
to-day, Henry, in the anthem when they sang it—'When
the Lord turned the captivity of Zion we were like them
that dream'—I thought, yes, like them that dream—them
that dream. And then it went on, 'They that sow in
tears shall reap in joy, and he that goeth forth and weep-
eth shall doubtless come home again with rejoicing, bringing his sheaves with him.' I looked up from the book
and saw you. I was not surprised when I saw you. I
knew you would come, my dear, and saw the gold sunshine round your head." And so it goes on running into
expressions of heart-melting tenderness. And yet she herself does not know that her own heart is seeking his with
all a woman's love. She is still willing that he should
possess Beatrix. "I would call you my son," she says,
"sooner than the greatest prince in Europe." But she
warns him of the nature of her own girl. "'Tis for my
poor Beatrix I tremble, whose headstrong will affrights
me, whose jealous temper, and whose vanity no prayers of
mine can cure." It is but very gradually that Esmond

becomes aware of the truth. Indeed, he has not become altogether aware of it till the tale closes. The reader does not see that transfer of affection from the daughter to the mother which would fail to reach his sympathy. In the last page of the last chapter it is told that it is so—that Esmond marries Lady Castlewood—but it is not told till all the incidents of the story have been completed.

But of the three characters I have named, Beatrix is the one that has most strongly exercised the writer's powers, and will most interest the reader. As far as outward person is concerned, she is very lovely—so charming that every man that comes near to her submits himself to her attractions and caprices. It is but rarely that a novelist can succeed in impressing his reader with a sense of female loveliness. The attempt is made so frequently—comes so much as a matter of course in every novel that is written, and fails so much as a matter of course, that the reader does not feel the failure. There are things which we do not expect to have done for us in literature, because they are done so seldom. Novelists are apt to describe the rural scenes among which their characters play their parts, but seldom leave any impression of the places described. Even in poetry how often does this occur? The words used are pretty, well chosen, perhaps musical to the ear, and in that way befitting; but unless the spot has violent characteristics of its own, such as Burley's cave or the waterfall of Lodore, no striking portrait is left. Nor are we disappointed as we read, because we have not been taught to expect it to be otherwise. So it is with those word-painted portraits of women, which are so frequently given and so seldom convey any impression. Who has an idea of the outside look of Sophia Western, or Edith Bellenden, or even of Imogen, though Iachimo, who described

her, was so good at words? A series of pictures—illustrations—as we have with Dickens' novels, and with Thackeray's, may leave an impression of a figure—though even
then not often of feminine beauty. But in this work
Thackeray has succeeded in imbuing us with a sense of
the outside loveliness of Beatrix by the mere force of
words. We are not only told it, but we feel that she was
such a one as a man cannot fail to covet, even when his
judgment goes against his choice.

Here the judgment goes altogether against the choice.
The girl grows up before us from her early youth till her
twenty-fifth or twenty-sixth year, and becomes — such as
her mother described her—one whose headlong will, whose
jealousy, and whose vanity nothing could restrain. She
has none of those soft foibles, half allied to virtues, by
which weak women fall away into misery or perhaps dis-
traction. She does not want to love or to be loved. She
does not care to be fondled. She has no longing for ca-
resses. She wants to be admired—and to make use of
the admiration she shall achieve for the material purposes
of her life. She wishes to rise in the world; and her
beauty is the sword with which she must open her oyster.
As to her heart, it is a thing of which she becomes aware,
only to assure herself that it must be laid aside and put
out of the question. Now and again Esmond touches it.
She just feels that she has a heart to be touched. But she
never has a doubt as to her conduct in that respect. She
will not allow her dreams of ambition to be disturbed by
such folly as love.

In all that there might be something, if not good and
great, nevertheless grand, if her ambition, though worldly,
had in it a touch of nobility. But this poor creature is
made with her bleared blind eyes to fall into the very

lowest depths of feminine ignobility. One lover comes
after another. Harry Esmond is, of course, the lover with
whom the reader interests himself. At last there comes
a duke—fifty years old, indeed, but with semi-royal appa-
nages. As his wife she will become a duchess, with many
diamonds, and be Her Excellency. The man is stern, cold,
and jealous; but she does not doubt for a moment. She
is to be Duchess of Hamilton, and towers already in pride
of place above her mother, and her kinsman lover, and all
her belongings. The story here, with its little incidents
of birth, and blood, and ignoble pride, and gratified ambition, with a dash of true feminine nobility on the part of
the girl's mother, is such as to leave one with the impression that it has hardly been beaten in English prose fiction. Then, in the last moment, the duke is killed in a
duel, and the news is brought to the girl by Esmond.
She turns upon him and rebukes him harshly. Then she
moves away, and feels in a moment that there is nothing
left for her in this world, and that she can only throw herself upon devotion for consolation. "I am best in my
own room and by myself," she said. Her eyes were quite
dry, nor did Esmond ever see them otherwise, save once,
in respect of that grief. She gave him a cold hand as she
went out. "Thank you, brother," she said in a low voice,
and with a simplicity more touching than tears; "all that
you have said is true and kind, and I will go away and
will ask pardon."

But the consolation coming from devotion did not go
far with such a one as her. We cannot rest on religion
merely by saying that we will do so. Very speedily there
comes consolation in another form. Queen Anne is on
her deathbed, and a young Stuart prince appears upon
the scene, of whom some loyal hearts dream that they

can make a king. He is such as Stuarts were, and only
walks across the novelist's canvas to show his folly and
heartlessness. But there is a moment in which Beatrix
thinks that she may rise in the world to the proud place
of a royal mistress. That is her last ambition! That is
her pride! That is to be her glory! The bleared eyes
can see no clearer than that. But the mock prince passes
away, and nothing but the disgrace of the wish remains.

Such is the story of *Esmond*, leaving with it, as does
all Thackeray's work, a melancholy conviction of the vanity of all things human. *Vanitas vanitatum*, as he wrote
on the pages of the French lady's album, and again in one
of the earlier numbers of *The Cornhill Magazine*. With
much that is picturesque, much that is droll, much that
is valuable as being a correct picture of the period selected, the gist of the book is melancholy throughout. It
ends with the promise of happiness to come, but that is
contained merely in a concluding paragraph. The one
woman, during the course of the story, becomes a widow,
with a living love in which she has no hope, with children
for whom her fears are almost stronger than her affection,
who never can rally herself to happiness for a moment.
The other, with all her beauty and all her brilliance, becomes what we have described—and marries at last her
brother's tutor, who becomes a bishop by means of her
intrigues. Esmond, the hero, who is compounded of all
good gifts, after a childhood and youth tinged throughout
with mélancholy, vanishes from us, with the promise that
he is to be rewarded by the hand of the mother of the
girl he has loved.

And yet there is not a page in the book over which a
thoughtful reader cannot pause with delight. The nature
in it is true nature. Given a story thus sad, and persons

thus situated, and it is thus that the details would follow each other, and thus that the people would conduct themselves. It was the tone of Thackeray's mind to turn away from the prospect of things joyful, and to see—or believe that he saw—in all human affairs, the seed of something base, of something which would be antagonistic to true contentment. All his snobs, and all his fools, and all his knaves, come from the same conviction. Is it not the doctrine on which our religion is founded—though the sadness of it there is alleviated by the doubtful promise of a heaven?

> Though thrice a thousand years are passed
> Since David's son, the sad and splendid,
> The weary king ecclesiast
> Upon his awful tablets penned it.

So it was that Thackeray preached his sermon. But melancholy though it be, the lesson taught in *Esmond* is salutary from beginning to end. The sermon truly preached is that glory can only come from that which is truly glorious, and that the results of meanness end always in the mean. No girl will be taught to wish to shine like Beatrix, nor will any youth be made to think that to gain the love of such a one it can be worth his while to expend his energy or his heart.

Esmond was published in 1852. It was not till 1858, some time after he had returned from his lecturing tours, that he published the sequel called *The Virginians*. It was first brought out in twenty-four monthly numbers, and ran through the years 1858 and 1859, Messrs. Bradbury and Evans having been the publishers. It takes up by no means the story of *Esmond*, and hardly the characters. The twin lads, who are called the Virginians, and

whose name is Warrington, are grandsons of Esmond and
his wife Lady Castlewood. Their one daughter, born at
the estate in Virginia, had married a Warrington, and the
Virginians are the issue of that marriage. In the story,
one is sent to England, there to make his way; and the
other is for awhile supposed to have been killed by the In-
dians. How he was not killed, but after awhile comes
again forward in the world of fiction, will be found in the
story, which it is not our purpose to set forth here. The
most interesting part of the narrative is that which tells
us of the later fortunes of Madame Beatrix—the Baroness
Bernstein—the lady who had in her youth been Beatrix
Esmond, who had then condescended to become Mrs.
Tusher, the tutor's wife, whence she rose to be the "lady"
of a bishop, and, after the bishop had been put to rest
under a load of marble, had become the baroness—a rich
old woman, courted by all her relatives because of her
wealth.

In *The Virginians*, as a work of art, is discovered, more
strongly than had shown itself yet in any of his works,
that propensity to wandering which came to Thackeray
because of his idleness. It is, I think, to be found in
every book he ever wrote—except *Esmond ;* but is here
more conspicuous than it had been in his earlier years.
Though he can settle himself down to his pen and ink—
not always even to that without a struggle, but to that
with sufficient burst of energy to produce a large average
amount of work—he cannot settle himself down to the
task of contriving a story. There have been those—
and they have not been bad judges of literature—who
have told me that they have best liked these vague narratives. The mind of the man has been clearly exhibited
in them. In them he has spoken out his thoughts, and

given the world to know his convictions, as well as could have been done in the carrying out any well-conducted plot. And though the narratives be vague, the characters are alive. In *The Virginians*, the two young men and their mother, and the other ladies with whom they have to deal, and especially their aunt, the Baroness Bernstein, are all alive. For desultory reading, for that picking up of a volume now and again which requires permission to forget the plot of a novel, this novel is admirably adapted. There is not a page of it vacant or dull. But he who takes it up to read as a whole, will find that it is the work of a desultory writer, to whom it is not unfrequently difficult to remember the incidents of his own narrative. "How good it is, even as it is!—but if he would have done his best for us, what might he not have done!" This, I think, is what we feel when we read *The Virginians*. The author's mind has in one way been active enough—and powerful, as it always is; but he has been unable to fix it to an intended purpose, and has gone on from day to day furthering the difficulty he has intended to master, till the book, under the stress of circumstances—demands for copy and the like—has been completed before the difficulty has even in truth been encountered.

CHAPTER VI.

THACKERAY'S BURLESQUES.

As so much of Thackeray's writing partakes of the nature
of burlesque, it would have been unnecessary to devote a
separate chapter to the subject, were it not that there are
among his tales two or three so exceedingly good of their
kind, coming so entirely up to our idea of what a prose
burlesque should be, that were I to omit to mention them
I should pass over a distinctive portion of our author's
work.

The volume called *Burlesques*, published in 1869, begins
with the *Novels by Eminent Hands*, and *Jeames's Diary*,
to which I have already alluded. It contains also *The
Tremendous Adventures of Major Gahagan*, *A Legend of
the Rhine*, and *Rebecca and Rowena*. It is of these that
I will now speak. *The History of the Next French Revolution* and *Cox's Diary*, with which the volume is concluded, are, according to my thinking, hardly equal to the
others; nor are they so properly called burlesques.

Nor will I say much of Major Gahagan, though his adventures are very good fun. He is a warrior—that is, of
course—and he is one in whose wonderful narrative all
that distant India can produce in the way of boasting,
is superadded to Ireland's best efforts in the same line.
Baron Munchausen was nothing to him; and to the bare

and simple miracles of the baron is joined that humour without which Thackeray never tells any story. This is broad enough, no doubt, but is still humour—as when the major tells us that he always kept in his own apartment a small store of gunpowder; "always keeping it under my bed, with a candle burning for fear of accidents." Or when he describes his courage; "I was running—running as the brave stag before the hounds—running, as I have done a great number of times in my life, when there was no help for it but a run." Then he tells us of his digestion. "Once in Spain I ate the leg of a horse, and was so eager to swallow this morsel, that I bolted the shoe as well as the hoof, and never felt the slightest inconvenience from either." He storms a citadel, and has only a snuff-box given him for his reward. "Never mind," says Major Gahagan; "when they want me to storm a fort again, I shall know better." By which we perceive that the major remembered his Horace, and had in his mind the soldier who had lost his purse. But the major's adventures, excellent as they are, lack the continued interest which is attached to the two following stories.

Of what nature is *The Legend of the Rhine*, we learn from the commencement. "It was in the good old days of chivalry, when every mountain that bathes its shadow in the Rhine had its castle; not inhabited as now by a few rats and owls, nor covered with moss and wallflowers and funguses and creeping ivy. No, no; where the ivy now clusters there grew strong portcullis and bars of steel; where the wallflowers now quiver in the ramparts there were silken banners embroidered with wonderful heraldry; men-at-arms marched where now you shall only see a bank of moss or a hideous black champignon; and in place of the rats and owlets, I warrant me there were ladies and

7

knights to revel in the great halls, and to feast and dance, and to make love there." So that we know well beforehand of what kind will this story be. It will be pure romance—burlesqued. "Ho seneschal, fill me a cup of hot liquor; put sugar in it, good fellow; yea, and a little hot water—but very little, for my soul is sad as I think of those days and knights of old."

A knight is riding alone on his war-horse, with all his armour with him—and his luggage. His rank is shown by the name on his portmanteau, and his former address and present destination by a card which was attached. It had run, "Count Ludwig de Hombourg, Jerusalem, but the name of the Holy City had been dashed out with the pen, and that of Godesberg substituted." "By St. Hugo of Katzenellenbogen," said the good knight, shivering, "'tis colder here than at Damascus. Shall I be at Godesberg in time for dinner?" He has come to see his friend Count Karl, Margrave of Godesberg.

But at Godesberg everything is in distress and sorrow. There is a new inmate there, one Sir Gottfried, since whose arrival the knight of the castle has become a wretched man, having been taught to believe all evils of his wife, and of his child Otto, and a certain stranger, one Hildebrandt. Gottfried, we see with half an eye, has done it all. It is in vain that Ludwig de Hombourg tells his old friend Karl that this Gottfried is a thoroughly bad fellow, that he had been found to be a card-sharper in the Holy Land, and had been drummed out of his regiment. "'Twas but some silly quarrel over the wine-cup," says Karl. "Hugo de Brodenel would have no black bottle on the board." We think we can remember the quarrel of "Brodenel" and the black bottle, though so many things have taken place since that.

There is a festival in the castle, and Hildebrandt comes with the other guests. Then Ludwig's attention is called by poor Karl, the father, to a certain family likeness. Can it be that he is not the father of his own child? He is playing cards with his friend Ludwig when that traitor Gottfried comes and whispers to him, and makes an appointment. "I will be there too," thought Count Ludwig, the good Knight of Hombourg.

On the next morning, before the stranger knight had shaken off his slumbers, all had been found out and everything done. The lady had been sent to a convent and her son to a monastery. The knight of the castle has no comfort but in his friend Gottfried, a distant cousin who is to inherit everything. All this is told to Sir Ludwig—who immediately takes steps to repair the mischief. "A cup of coffee straight," says he to the servitors. "Bid the cook pack me a sausage and bread in paper, and the groom saddle Streithengst. We have far to ride." So this redresser of wrongs starts off, leaving the Margrave in his grief.

Then there is a great fight between Sir Ludwig and Sir Gottfried, admirably told in the manner of the later chroniclers—a hermit sitting by and describing everything almost as well as Rebecca did on the tower. Sir Ludwig being in the right, of course gains the day. But the escape of the fallen knight's horse is the cream of this chapter. "Away, ay, away!—away amid the green vineyards and golden cornfields; away up the steep mountains, where he frightened the eagles in their eyries; away down the clattering ravines, where the flashing cataracts tumble; away through the dark pine-forests, where the hungry wolves are howling; away over the dreary wolds, where the wild wind walks alone; away through the splashing

K   10

quagmires, where the will-o'-the wisp slunk frightened
among the reeds; away through light and darkness, storm
and sunshine; away by tower and town, highroad and
hamlet. . . . Brave horse! gallant steed! snorting child of
Aiaby! On went the horse, over mountains, rivers, turn-
pikes, applewomen; and never stopped until he reached a
livery-stable in Cologne, where his master was accustomed
to put him up!"

The conquered knight, Sir Gottfried, of course reveals
the truth. This Hildebrandt is no more than the lady's
brother—as it happened a brother in disguise—and hence
the likeness. Wicked knights, when they die, always di-
vulge their wicked secrets, and this knight Gottfried does
so now. Sir Ludwig carries the news home to the afflict-
ed husband and father; who of course instantly sends off
messengers for his wife and son. The wife won't come.
All she wants is to have her dresses and jewels sent to her.
Of so cruel a husband she has had enough. As for the
son, he has jumped out of a boat on the Rhine, as he was
being carried to his monastery, and was drowned!

But he was not drowned, but had only dived. "The
gallant boy swam on beneath the water, never lifting his
head for a single moment between Godesberg and Cologne;
the distance being twenty-five or thirty miles."

Then he becomes an archer, dressed in green from head
to foot. How it was is all told in the story; and he goes
to shoot for a prize at the Castle of Adolf the Duke of
Cleeves. On his way he shoots a raven marvellously—almost as marvellously as did Robin Hood the twig in Ivanhoe. Then one of his companions is married, or nearly
married, to the mysterious "Lady of Windeck"—would
have been married but for Otto, and that the bishop and
dean, who were dragged up from their long-ago graves to

perform the ghostly ceremony, were prevented by the ill-timed mirth of a certain old canon of the church named Schidnischmidt. The reader has to read the name out loud before he recognizes an old friend. But this of the Lady of Windeck is an episode.

How at the shooting - match, which of course ensued, Otto shot for and won the heart of a fair lady, the duke's daughter, need not be told here, nor how he quarrelled with the Rowski of Donnerblitz—the hideous and sulky, but rich and powerful, nobleman who had come to take the hand, whether he could win the heart or not, of the daughter of the duke. It is all arranged according to the proper and romantic order. Otto, though he enlists in the duke's archer-guard as simple soldier, contrives to fight with the Rowski de Donnerblitz, Margrave of Eulenschren-kenstein, and of course kills him. "'Yield, yield, Sir Rowski!' shouted he, in a calm voice. A blow dealt madly at his head was the reply. It was the last blow that the Count of Eulenschrenkenstein ever struck in battle. The curse was on his lips as the crashing steel descended into his brain and split it in two. He rolled like a dog from his horse, his enemy's knee was in a moment on his chest, and the dagger of mercy at his throat, as the knight once more called upon him to yield." The knight was of course the archer who had come forward as an unknown champion, and had touched the Rowski's shield with the point of his lance. For this story, as well as the rest, is a burlesque on our dear old favourite Ivanhoe.

That everything goes right at last, that the wife comes back from her monastery, and joins her jealous husband, and that the duke's daughter has always, in truth, known that the poor archer was a noble knight—these things are all matters of course.

But the best of the three burlesques is *Rebecca and Rowena, or A Romance upon Romance,* which I need not tell my readers is a continuation of *Ivanhoe.* Of this burlesque it is the peculiar characteristic that, while it has been written to ridicule the persons and the incidents of that perhaps the most favourite novel in the English language, it has been so written that it would not have offended the author had he lived to read it, nor does it disgust or annoy those who most love the original. There is not a word in it having an intention to belittle Scott. It has sprung from the genuine humour created in Thackeray's mind by his aspect of the romantic. We remember how reticent, how dignified was Rowena—how cold we perhaps thought her, whether there was so little of that billing and cooing, that kissing and squeezing, between her and Ivanhoe which we used to think necessary to lovers' blisses. And there was left, too, on our minds an idea that Ivanhoe had liked the Jewess almost as well as Rowena, and that Rowena might possibly have become jealous. Thackeray's mind at once went to work and pictured to him a Rowena such as such a woman might become after marriage; and as Ivanhoe was of a melancholy nature and apt to be hipped, and grave, and silent, as a matter of course Thackeray presumes him to have been henpecked after his marriage.

Our dear Wamba disturbs his mistress in some devotional conversation with her chaplain, and the stern lady orders that the fool shall have three-dozen lashes. "I got you out of Front de Bœuf's castle," said poor Wamba, piteously appealing to Sir Wilfrid of Ivanhoe, "and canst thou not save me from the lash?"

"Yes; from Front de Bœuf's castle, *when you were locked up with the Jewess in the tower!*" said Rowena, haughtily replying to the timid appeal of her husband.

"Gurth, give him four-dozen"—and this was all poor
Wamba got by applying for the mediation of his master.
Then the satirist moralises: "Did you ever know a right-
minded woman pardon another for being handsomer and
more love-worthy than herself?" Rowena is "always
flinging Rebecca into Ivanhoe's teeth;" and altogether life
at Rotherwood, as described by the later chronicles, is not
very happy even when most domestic. Ivanhoe becomes
sad and moody. He takes to drinking, and his lady does
not forget to tell him of it. "Ah, dear axe!" he exclaims,
apostrophising his weapon, "ah, gentle steel! that was a
merry time when I sent thee crashing into the pate of the
Emir Abdul Melek!" There was nothing left to him but
his memories; and "in a word, his life was intolerable."
So he determines that he will go and look after King
Richard, who of course was wandering abroad. He antici-
pates a little difficulty with his wife; but she is only too
happy to let him go, comforting herself with the idea that
Athelstane will look after her. So her husband starts on
his journey. "Then Ivanhoe's trumpet blew. Then Rowena waved her pocket-handkerchief. Then the household
gave a shout. Then the pursuivant of the good knight,
Sir Wilfrid the Crusader, flung out his banner—which
was argent, a gules cramoisy with three Moors impaled—
then Wamba gave a lash on his mule's haunch, and Ivanhoe, heaving a great sigh, turned the tail of his war-horse
upon the castle of his fathers."

Ivanhoe finds Cœur de Leon besieging the Castle of
Chalons, and there they both do wondrous deeds, Ivanhoe
always surpassing the king. The jealousy of the courtiers,
the ingratitude of the king, and the melancholy of the
knight, who is never comforted except when he has slaugh-
tered some hundreds, are delightful. Roger de Backbite

and Peter de Toadhole are intended to be quite real. Then his majesty sings, passing off as his own a song of Charles Lever's. Sir Wilfrid declares the truth, and twits the king with his falsehood, whereupon he has the guitar thrown at his head for his pains. He catches the guitar, however, gracefully in his left hand, and sings his own immortal ballad of *King Canute*—than which Thackeray never did anything better.

"Might I stay the sun above us, good Sir Bishop?" Canute cried;
"Could I bid the silver moon to pause upon her heavenly ride?
If the moon obeys my orders, sure I can command the tide.

Will the advancing waves obey me, Bishop, if I make the sign?"
Said the bishop, bowing lowly: "Land and sea, my lord, are thine."
Canute turned towards the ocean: "Back," he said, "thou foaming
    brine."

But the sullen ocean answered with a louder, deeper roar,
And the rapid waves drew nearer, falling, sounding on the shore;
Back the keeper and the bishop, back the king and courtiers bore.

We must go to the book to look at the picture of the king as he is killing the youngest of the sons of the Count of Chalons. Those illustrations of Doyle's are admirable. The size of the king's head, and the size of his battle-axe as contrasted with the size of the child, are burlesque all over. But the king has been wounded by a bolt from the bow of Sir Bertrand de Gourdon while he is slaughtering the infant, and there is an end of him. Ivanhoe, too, is killed at the siege—Sir Roger de Backbite having stabbed him in the back during the scene. Had he not been then killed, his widow Rowena could not have married Athelstane, which she soon did after hearing the sad news; nor could he have had that celebrated epitaph in Latin and English:

Hic est Guilfridus, belli dum vixit avidus.
Cum gladeo et lancea Normannia et quoque Francia
Verbera dura dabat. Per Turcos multum equitabat.
Guilbertum occidit ;—atque Hyerosolyma vidit.
Heu ! nunc sub fossa sunt tanti militis ossa.
Uxor Athelstani est conjux castissima Thani.[1]

The translation, we are told, was by Wamba :

Under the stone you behold,
Buried and coffined and cold,
Lieth Sir Wilfrid the Bold.

Brian, the Templar untrue,
Fairly in tourney he slew ;
Saw Hierusalem too.

Always he marched in advance,
Warring in Flanders and France,
Doughty with sword and with
lance.

Now he is buried and gone,
Lying beneath the gray stone.
Where shall you find such a
one ?

Famous in Saracen fight,
Rode in his youth, the Good
Knight,
Scattering Paynims in flight.

Long time his widow deplored,
Weeping, the fate of her lord,
Sadly cut off by the sword.

When she was eased of her pain,
Came the good lord Athelstane,
When her ladyship married again.

The next chapter begins naturally as follows : "I trust
nobody will suppose, from the events described in the last
chapter, that our friend Ivanhoe is really dead."   He is of
course cured of his wounds, though they take six years in
the curing.   And then he makes his way back to Rotherwood, in a friar's disguise, much as he did on that former

[1] I doubt that Thackeray did not write the Latin epitaph, but I
hardly dare suggest the name of any author. The "vixit avidus"
is quite worthy of Thackeray ; but had he tried his hand at such
mode of expression he would have done more of it. I should like to
know whether he had been in company with Father Prout at the time.

7*

occasion when we first met him, and there is received by
Athelstane and Rowena—and their boy!—while Wamba
sings him a song:

> Then you know the worth of a lass,
> Once you have come to forty year!

No one, of course, but Wamba knows Ivanhoe, who
roams about the country, melancholy—as he of course
would be—charitable—as he perhaps might be—for we
are specially told that he had a large fortune and nothing
to do with it, and slaying robbers wherever he met them—
but sad at heart all the time. Then there comes a little
burst of the author's own feelings, while he is burlesquing.
"Ah my dear friends and British public, are there not others who are melancholy under a mask of gaiety, and who
in the midst of crowds are lonely? Liston was a most
melancholy man; Grimaldi had feelings; and then others
I wot of. But psha!—let us have the next chapter." In
all of which there was a touch of earnestness.

Ivanhoe's griefs were enhanced by the wickedness of
King John, under whom he would not serve. "It was Sir
Wilfrid of Ivanhoe, I need scarcely say, who got the Bar-
ons of England to league together and extort from the
king that famous instrument and palladium of our liberties, at present in the British Museum, Great Russell Street,
Bloomsbury—The Magna Charta." Athelstane also quarrels with the king, whose orders he disobeys, and Rotherwood is attacked by the royal army. No one was of real
service in the way of fighting except Ivanhoe—and how
could he take up that cause? "No; be hanged to me,"
said the knight, bitterly. "This is a quarrel in which I
can't interfere. Common politeness forbids. Let yonder
ale-swilling Athelstane defend his— ha, ha!— *wife;* and

my Lady Rowena guard her — ha, ha!—*son!*" and he laughed wildly and madly.

But Athelstane is killed—this time in earnest—and then Ivanhoe rushes to the rescue. He finds Gurth dead at the park-lodge; and though he is all alone—having out ridden his followers — he rushes up the chestnut avenue to the house, which is being attacked. "An Ivanhoe! an Ivanhoe!" he bellowed out with a shout that overcame all the din of battle;—"Notre Dame à la recousse!" and to hurl his lance through the midriff of Reginald de Bracy, who was commanding the assault—who fell howling with anguish—to wave his battle-axe over his own head, and to cut off those of thirteen men-at-arms, was the work of an instant. "An Ivanhoe! an Ivanhoe!" he still shouted, and down went a man as sure as he said "hoe!"

Nevertheless he is again killed by multitudes, or very nearly—and has again to be cured by the tender nursing of Wamba. But Athelstane is really dead, and Rowena and the boy have to be found. He does his duty and finds them—just in time to be present at Rowena's death. She has been put in prison by King John, and is in extremis when her first husband gets to her. "Wilfrid, my early loved,"[1] slowly gasped she, removing her gray hair from her furrowed temples, and gazing on her boy fondly as he nestled on Ivanhoe's knee—"promise me by St. Waltheof of Templestowe—promise me one boon!"

"I do," said Ivanhoe, clasping the boy, and thinking that it was to that little innocent that the promise was intended to apply.

[1] There is something almost illnatured in his treatment of Rowena, who is very false in her declarations of love;—and it is to be feared that by Rowena the author intends the normal married lady of English society.

" By St. Waltheof ?"

" By St. Waltheof !"

" Promise me, then," gasped Rowena, staring wildly at him, " that you will never marry a Jewess !"

" By St. Waltheof !" cried Ivanhoe, " but this is too much," and he did not make the promise.

"Having placed young Cedric at school at the Hall of Dotheboys, in Yorkshire, and arranged his family affairs, Sir Wilfrid of Ivanhoe quitted a country which had no longer any charm for him, as there was no fighting to be done, and in which his stay was rendered less agreeable by the notion that King John would hang him." So he goes forth and fights again, in league with the Knights of St. John—the Templars naturally having a dislike to him because of Brian de Bois Guilbert. " The only fault that the great and gallant, though severe and ascetic Folko of Heydenbraten, the chief of the Order of St. John, found with the melancholy warrior whose lance did such service to the cause, was that he did not persecute the Jews as so religious a knight should. So the Jews, in cursing the Christians, always excepted the name of the Desdichado —or the double disinherited, as he now was — the Desdichado Doblado." Then came the battle of Alarcos, and the Moors were all but in possession of the whole of Spain. Sir Wilfrid, like other good Christians, cannot endure this, so he takes ship in Bohemia, where he happens to be quartered, and has himself carried to Barcelona, and proceeds " to slaughter the Moors forthwith." Then there is a scene in which Isaac of York comes on as a messenger, to ransom from a Spanish knight, Don Beltram de Cuchilla y Trabuco, y Espada, y Espelon, a little Moorish girl. The Spanish knight of course murders the little girl instead of taking the ransom. Two hundred thousand dirhems are offered, however much that may be; but the knight, who happens to be in funds at the time, prefers to kill the little girl. All this is only necessary to the story as introducing Isaac of York. Sir Wilfrid is of course intent upon finding Rebecca. Through all his troubles and triumphs, from his gaining and his losing of Rowena, from the day on which he had been "*locked up with the Jewess in the tower*," he had always been true to her. "Away from me!" said the old Jew, tottering. "Away, Rebecca is — dead!" Then Ivanhoe goes out and kills fifty thousand Moors, and there is the picture of him — killing them.

But Rebecca is not dead at all. Her father had said so because Rebecca had behaved very badly to him. She had refused to marry the Moorish prince, or any of her own people, the Jews, and had gone as far as to declare her passion for Ivanhoe and her resolution to be a Christian. All the Jews and Jewesses in Valencia turned against her—so that she was locked up in the back-kitchen and almost starved to death. But Ivanhoe found her, of course, and makes her Mrs. Ivanhoe, or Lady Wilfrid the second. Then Thackeray tells us how for many years he, Thackeray, had not ceased to feel that it ought to be so. "Indeed I have thought of it any time these five-and-twenty years—ever since, as a boy at school, I commenced the noble study of novels—ever since the day when, lying on sunny slopes, of half-holidays, the fair chivalrous figures and beautiful shapes of knights and ladies were visible to me, ever since I grew to love Rebecca, that sweetest creature of the poet's fancy, and longed to see her righted."

And so, no doubt, it had been. The very burlesque had grown from the way in which his young imagination had been moved by Scott's romance. He had felt, from the time of those happy half-holidays in which he had been lucky enough to get hold of the novel, that according to all laws of poetic justice, Rebecca, as being the more beautiful and the more interesting of the heroines, was entitled to the possession of the hero. We have all of us felt the same. But to him had been present at the same time all that is ludicrous in our ideas of middle-age chivalry; the absurdity of its recorded deeds, the blood-thirstiness of its recreations, the selfishness of its men, the falseness of its honour, the cringing of its loyalty, the tyranny of its princes. And so there came forth Rebecca and Rowena, all broad fun from beginning to end, but never without a purpose—the best burlesque, as I think, in our language.

CHAPTER VII.

In speaking of Thackeray's life, I have said why and how it was that he took upon himself to lecture, and have also told the reader that he was altogether successful in carrying out the views proposed to himself. Of his peculiar manner of lecturing I have said but little, never having heard him. "He pounded along—very clearly," I have been told; from which I surmise that there was no special grace of eloquence, but that he was always audible. I cannot imagine that he should have been ever eloquent. He could not have taken the trouble necessary with his voice, with his cadences, or with his outward appearance. I imagine that they who seem so naturally to fall into the proprieties of elocution have generally taken a great deal of trouble beyond that which the mere finding of their words has cost them. It is clearly to the matter of what he then gave the world, and not to the manner, that we must look for what interest is to be found in the lectures.

Those on *The English Humorists* were given first. The second set was on *The Four Georges.* In the volume now before us *The Georges* are printed first, and the whole is produced simply as a part of Thackeray's literary work. Looked at, however, in that light, the merit of the two sets of biographical essays is very different. In the

one we have all the anecdotes which could be brought together respecting four of our kings — who as men were
not peculiar, though their reigns were, and will always be,
famous, because the country during the period was in-
creasing greatly in prosperity, and was ever strengthening
the hold it had upon its liberties. In the other set the
lecturer was a man of letters dealing with men of letters,
and himself a prince among humorists is dealing with the
humorists of his own country and language. One could
not imagine a better subject for such discourses from
Thackeray's mouth than the latter. The former was not,
I think, so good.

In discussing the lives of kings the biographer may
trust to personal details or to historical facts. He may
take the man, and say what good or evil may be said of
him as a man;—or he may take the period, and tell his
readers what happened to the country while this or the
other king was on the throne. In the case with which
we are dealing, the lecturer had not time enough or room
enough for real history. His object was to let his audience know of what nature were the men ; and we are bound
to say that the pictures have not, on the whole, been flattering. It was almost necessary that with such a subject
such should be the result. A story of family virtues, with
princes and princesses well brought up, with happy family
relations, all couleur de rose — as it would of course become us to write if we were dealing with the life of a
living sovereign—would not be interesting. No one on
going to hear Thackeray lecture on the Georges expected
that. There must be some piquancy given, or the lecture
would be dull;—and the eulogy of personal virtues can seldom be piquant. It is difficult to speak fittingly of a sovereign, either living or not, long since gone. You can

hardly praise such a one without flattery. You can hardly censure him without injustice. We are either ignorant of his personal doings or we know them as secrets, which have been divulged for the most part either falsely or treacherously — often both falsely and treacherously. It is better, perhaps, that we should not deal with the personalities of princes.

I believe that Thackeray fancied that he had spoken well of George III., and am sure that it was his intention to do so. But the impression he leaves is poor. " He is said not to have cared for Shakespeare or tragedy much; farces and pantomimes were his joy;—and especially when clown swallowed a carrot or a string of sausages, he would laugh so outrageously that the lovely princess by his side would have to say, 'My gracious monarch, do compose yourself.' 'George, be a king!' were the words which she "—his mother—" was ever croaking in the ears of her son ; and a king the simple, stubborn, affectionate, bigoted man tried to be." "He did his best; he worked according to his lights; what virtues he knew he tried to practise; what knowledge he could master he strove to acquire." If the lectures were to be popular, it was absolutely necessary that they should be written in this strain. A lecture simply laudatory on the life of St. Paul would not draw even the bench of bishops to listen to it ; but were a flaw found in the apostle's life, the whole Church of England would be bound to know all about it. I am quite sure that Thackeray believed every word that he said in the lectures, and that he intended to put in the good and the bad, honestly, as they might come to his hand. We may be quite sure that he did not intend to flatter the royal family ;—equally sure that he would not calumniate. There were, however, so many difficulties to be encountered that I cannot but think that the subject was ill-chosen. In making them so amusing as he did, and so little offensive, great ingenuity was shown.

I will now go back to the first series, in which the lecturer treated of Swift, Congreve, Addison, Steele, Prior, Gay, Pope, Hogarth, Smollett, Fielding, Sterne, and Goldsmith. All these Thackeray has put in their proper order, placing the men from the date of their birth, except Prior, who was in truth the eldest of the lot, but whom it was necessary to depose, in order that the great Swift might stand first on the list, and Smollett, who was not born till fourteen years after Fielding, eight years after Sterne, and who has been moved up, I presume, simply from caprice. From the birth of the first to the death of the last, was a period of nearly a hundred years. They were never absolutely all alive together; but it was nearly so, Addison and Prior having died before Smollett was born. Whether we should accept as humorists the full catalogue, may be a question; though we shall hardly wish to eliminate any one from such a dozen of names. Pope we should hardly define as a humorist, were we to be seeking for a definition specially fit for him, though we shall certainly not deny the gift of humour to the author of *The Rape of the Lock*, or to the translator of any portion of *The Odyssey*. Nor should we have included Fielding or Smollett, in spite of Parson Adams and Tabitha Bramble, unless anxious to fill a good company. That Hogarth was specially a humorist no one will deny; but in speaking of humorists we should have presumed, unless otherwise notified, that humorists in letters only had been intended. As Thackeray explains clearly what he means by a humorist, I may as well here repeat the passage: "If humour only meant laughter, you would scarcely feel more

interest about humorous writers than about the private
life of poor Harlequin just mentioned, who possesses in
common with these the power of making you laugh. But
the men regarding whose lives and stories your kind presence here shows that you have curiosity and sympathy,
appeal to a great number of our other faculties, besides
our mere sense of ridicule. The humorous writer pro-
fesses to awaken and direct your love, your pity, your
kindness—your scorn for untruth, pretension, imposture—
your tenderness for the weak, the poor, the oppressed, the
unhappy. To the best of his means and ability he comments on all the ordinary actions and passions of life almost. He takes upon himself to be the week-day preacher, so to speak. Accordingly, as he finds, and speaks, and
feels the truth best, we regard him, esteem him—sometimes love him. And as his business is to mark other
people's lives and peculiarities, we moralise upon *his* life
when he is gone—and yesterday's preacher becomes the
text for to-day's sermon."

Having thus explained his purpose, Thackeray begins
his task, and puts Swift in his front rank as a humorist.
The picture given of this great man has very manifestly
the look of truth, and if true, is terrible indeed. We do,
in fact, know it to be true—even though it be admitted
that there is still room left for a book to be written on
the life of the fearful dean. Here was a man endued with
an intellect pellucid as well as brilliant; who could not
only conceive but see also—with some fine instincts too;
whom fortune did not flout; whom circumstances fairly
served; but who, from first to last, was miserable himself,
who made others miserable, and who deserved misery.
Our business, during the page or two which we can give
to the subject, is not with Swift, but with Thackeray's

picture of Swift. It is painted with colours terribly strong and with shadows fearfully deep. "Would you like to have lived with him?" Thackeray asks. Then he says how pleasant it would have been to have passed some time with Fielding, Johnson, or Goldsmith. "I should like to have been Shakespeare's shoeblack," he says. "But Swift! If you had been his inferior in parts—and that, with a great respect for all persons present, I fear is only very likely—his equal in mere social station, he would have bullied, scorned, and insulted you. If, undeterred by his great reputation, you had met him like a man, he would have quailed before you and not had the pluck to reply—and gone home, and years after written a foul epigram upon you." There is a picture! "If you had been a lord with a blue riband, who flattered his vanity, or could help his ambition, he would have been the most delightful company in the world. . . . How he would have torn your enemies to pieces for you, and made fun of the Opposition! His servility was so boisterous that it looked like independence." He was a man whose mind was never fixed on high things, but was striving always after something which, little as it might be, and successful as he was, should always be out of his reach. It had been his misfortune to become a clergyman, because the way to church preferment seemed to be the readiest. He became, as we all know, a dean—but never a bishop, and was therefore wretched. Thackeray describes him as a clerical highwayman, seizing on all he could get. But "the great prize has not yet come. The coach with the mitre and crozier in it, which he intends to have for *his* share, has been delayed on the way from St. James's; and he waits and waits till nightfall, when his runners come and tell him that the coach has taken a different way and escaped him.

So he fires his pistol into the air with a curse, and rides away into his own country;"—or, in other words, takes a poor deanery in Ireland.

Thackeray explains very correctly, as I think, the nature of the weapons which the man used—namely, the words and style with which he wrote. "That Swift was born at No. 7, Hoey's Court, Dublin, on November 30, 1667, is a certain fact, of which nobody will deny the sister-island the honour and glory; but it seems to me he was no more an Irishman than a man born of English parents at Calcutta is a Hindoo. Goldsmith was an Irishman, and always an Irishman; Steele was an Irishman, and always an Irishman; Swift's heart was English and in England, his habits English, his logic eminently English; his statement is elaborately simple; he shuns tropes and metaphors, and uses his ideas and words with a wise thrift and economy, as he used his money;—with which he could be generous and splendid upon great occasions, but which he husbanded when there was no need to spend it. He never indulges in needless extravagance of rhetoric, lavish epithets, profuse imagery. He lays his opinions before you with a grave simplicity and a perfect neatness." This is quite true of him, and the result is that though you may deny him sincerity, simplicity, humanity, or good taste, you can hardly find fault with his language.

Swift was a clergyman, and this is what Thackeray says of him in regard to his sacred profession. "I know of few things more conclusive as to the sincerity of Swift's religion, than his advice to poor John Gay to turn clergyman, and look out for a seat on the Bench! Gay, the author of *The Beggar's Opera;* Gay, the wildest of the wits about town! It was this man that Jonathan Swift advised to take orders, to mount in a cassock and bands—

just as he advised him to husband his shillings, and put
his thousand pounds out to interest."

It was not that he was without religion—or without,
rather, his religious beliefs and doubts, "for Swift," says
Thackeray, "was a reverent, was a pious spirit. For Swift
could love and could pray." Left to himself and to the
natural thoughts of his mind, without those "orders" to
which he had bound himself as a necessary part of his
trade, he could have turned to his God with questionings
which need not then have been heartbreaking. "It is my
belief," says Thackeray, "that he suffered frightfully from
the consciousness of his own scepticism, and that he had
bent his pride so far down as to put his apostasy out to
hire." I doubt whether any of Swift's works are very
much read now, but perhaps Gulliver's travels are oftener
in the hands of modern readers than any other. Of all
the satires in our language, it is probably the most cynical,
the most absolutely illnatured, and therefore the falsest.
Let those who care to form an opinion of Swift's mind
from the best known of his works, turn to Thackeray's
account of Gulliver. I can imagine no greater proof of
misery than to have been able to write such a book as that.

It is thus that the lecturer concludes his lecture about
Swift: "He shrank away from all affections sooner or
later. Stella and Vanessa both died near him, and away
from him. He had not heart enough to see them die.
He broke from his fastest friend, Sheridan. He slunk
away from his fondest admirer, Pope. His laugh jars on
one's ear after seven-score years. He was always alone—
alone and gnashing in the darkness, except when Stella's
sweet smile came and shone on him. When that went,
silence and utter night closed over him. An immense
genius, an awful downfall and ruin! So great a man he

seems to me, that thinking of him is like thinking of an empire falling. We have other great names to mention— none, I think, however, so great or so gloomy." And so we pass on from Swift, feeling that though the man was certainly a humorist, we have had as yet but little to do with humour.

Congreve is the next who, however truly he may have been a humorist, is described here rather as a man of fashion. A man of fashion he certainly was, but is best known in our literature as a comedian—worshipping that Comic Muse to whom Thackeray hesitates to introduce his audience, because she is not only merry, but shameless also. Congreve's muse was about as bad as any muse that ever misbehaved herself—and I think, as little amusing. "Reading in these plays now," says Thackeray, "is like shutting your ears and looking at people dancing. What does it mean ?—the measures, the grimaces, the bowing, shuffling, and retreating, the cavaliers seul advancing upon those ladies—those ladies and men twirling round at the end in a mad galop, after which everybody bows and the quaint rite is celebrated ?" It is always so with Congreve's plays, and Etherege's and Wycherley's. The world we meet there is not our world, and as we read the plays we have no sympathy with these unknown people. It was not that they lived so long ago. They are much nearer to us in time than the men and women who figured on the stage in the reign of James I. But their nature is farther from our nature. They sparkle, but never warm. They are witty, but leave no impression. I might almost go further, and say that they are wicked, but never allure. "When Voltaire came to visit the great Congreve," says Thackeray, "the latter rather affected to despise his literary reputation; and in this, perhaps, the great Congreve was not far wrong. A touch of Steele's tenderness is worth all his finery; a flash of Swift's lightning, a beam of Addison's pure sunshine, and his tawdry playhouse taper is invisible. But the ladies loved him, and he was undoubtedly a pretty fellow."

There is no doubt as to the true humour of Addison, who next comes up before us, but I think that he makes hardly so good a subject for a lecturer as the great gloomy man of intellect, or the frivolous man of pleasure. Thackeray tells us all that is to be said about him as a humorist in so few lines that I may almost insert them on this page: "But it is not for his reputation as the great author of *Cato* and *The Campaign*, or for his merits as Secretary of State, or for his rank and high distinction as Lady Warwick's husband, or for his eminence as an examiner of political questions on the Whig side, or a guardian of British liberties, that we admire Joseph Addison. It is as a Tattler of small talk and a Spectator of mankind that we cherish and love him, and owe as much pleasure to him as to any human being that ever wrote. He came in that artificial age, and began to speak with his noble natural voice. He came the gentle satirist, who hit no unfair blow; the kind judge, who castigated only in smiling. While Swift went about hanging and ruthless, a literary Jeffreys, in Addison's kind court only minor cases were tried; — only peccadilloes and small sins against society, only a dangerous libertinism in tuckers and hoops, or a nuisance in the abuse of beaux canes and snuffboxes." Steele set *The Tatler* a-going. "But with his friend's discovery of *The Tatler*, Addison's calling was found, and the most delightful Tattler in the world began to speak. He does not go very deep. Let gentlemen of a profound genius, critics accustomed to the plunge of the bathes, con

sole themselves by thinking that he couldn't go very deep.
There is no trace of suffering in his writing. He was so
good, so honest, so healthy, so cheerfully selfish—if I must
use the word!"

Such was Addison as a humorist; and when the hearer
shall have heard also—or the reader read—that this most
charming Tattler also wrote *Cato*, became a Secretary of
State, and married a countess, he will have learned all that
Thackeray had to tell of him.

Steele was one who stood much less high in the world's
esteem, and who left behind him a much smaller name—
but was quite Addison's equal as a humorist and a wit.
Addison, though he had the reputation of a toper, was re-
spectability itself. Steele was almost always disreputable.
He was brought from Ireland, placed at the Charter House,
and then transferred to Oxford, where he became acquainted with Addison. Thackeray says that "Steele found Addison a stately college don at Oxford." The stateliness
and the don's rank were attributable no doubt to the more
sober character of the English lad, for, in fact, the two
men were born in the same year, 1672. Steele, who during
his life was affected by various different tastes, first turned
himself to literature, but early in life was bitten by the hue
of a red coat and became a trooper in the Horse Guards.
To the end he vacillated in the same way. In that charming paper in *The Tatler*, in which he records his father's
death, his mother's griefs, his own most solemn and tender emotions, he says he is interrupted by the arrival of a
hamper of wine, ' the same as is to be sold at Garraway's
next week ;' upon the receipt of which he sends for three
friends, and they fall to instantly, drinking two bottles
apiece, with great benefit to themselves, and not separating
till two o'clock in the morning."

8

He had two wives, whom he loved dearly and treated badly. He hired grand houses, and bought fine horses for which he could never pay. He was often religious, but more often drunk. As a man of letters, other men of letters who followed him, such as Thackeray, could not be very proud of him. But everybody loved him; and he seems to have been the inventor of that flying literature which, with many changes in form and manner, has done so much for the amusement and edification of readers ever since his time. He was always commencing, or carrying on—often editing—some one of the numerous periodicals which appeared during his time. Thackeray mentions seven: *The Tatler, The Spectator, The Guardian, The Englishman, The Lover, The Reader,* and *The Theatre;* that three of them are well known to this day—the three first named—and are to be found in all libraries, is proof that his life was not thrown away.

I almost question Prior's right to be in the list, unless, indeed, the mastery over well-turned conceits is to be included within the border of humour. But Thackeray had a strong liking for Prior, and in his own humorous way rebukes his audience for not being familiar with *The Town and Country Mouse.* He says that Prior's epigrams have the genuine sparkle, and compares Prior to Horace. "His song, his philosophy, his good sense, his happy, easy turns and melody, his loves and his epicureanism, bear a great resemblance to that most delightful and accomplished master." I cannot say that I agree with this. Prior is generally neat in his expression. Horace is happy—which is surely a great deal more.

All that is said of Gay, Pope, Hogarth, Smollett, and Fielding is worth reading, and may be of great value both to those who have not time to study the authors, and to those who desire to have their own judgments somewhat guided, somewhat assisted. That they were all men of humour there can be no doubt. Whether either of them, except perhaps Gay, would have been specially ranked as a humorist among men of letters, may be a question.

Sterne was a humorist, and employed his pen in that line, if ever a writer did so, and so was Goldsmith. Of the excellence and largeness of the disposition of the one, and the meanness and littleness of the other, it is not necessary that I should here say much. But I will give a short passage from our author as to each. He has been quoting somewhat at length from Sterne, and thus he ends: "And with this pretty dance and chorus the volume artfully concludes. Even here one can't give the whole description. There is not a page in Sterne's writing but has something that were better away, a latent corruption—a hint as of an impure presence. Some of that dreary double entendre may be attributed to freer times and manners than ours — but not all. The foul satyr's eyes leer out of the leaves constantly. The last words the famous author wrote were bad and wicked. The last lines the poor stricken wretch penned were for pity and pardon." Now a line or two about Goldsmith, and I will then let my reader go to the volume and study the lectures for himself. "The poor fellow was never so friendless but that he could befriend some one; never so pinched and wretched but he could give of his crust, and speak his word of compassion. If he had but his flute left, he would give that, and make the children happy in the dreary London courts."

Of this, too, I will remind my readers—those who have bookshelves well-filled to adorn their houses—that Goldsmith stands in the front where all the young people see

the volumes.   There are few among the young people who
do not refresh their sense of humour occasionally from
that shelf; Sterne is relegated to some distant and high
corner.   The less often that he is taken down the better.
Thackeray makes some half excuse for him because of the
greater freedom of the times.   But "the times" were the
same for the two.   Both Sterne and Goldsmith wrote
in the reign of George II.; both died in the reign of
George III.

CHAPTER VIII.

THACKERAY'S BALLADS.

WE have a volume of Thackeray's poems, republished under the name of *Ballads*, which is, I think, to a great extent
a misnomer. They are all readable, almost all good, full of
humour, and with some fine touches of pathos, most happy
in their versification, and, with a few exceptions, hitting
well on the head the nail which he intended to hit. But
they are not on that account ballads. Literally, a ballad
is a song; but it has come to signify a short chronicle in
verse, which may be political, or pathetic, or grotesque—
or it may have all three characteristics or any two of them;
but not on that account is any grotesque poem a ballad—
nor, of course, any pathetic or any political poem. *Jacob
Omnium's Hoss* may fairly be called a ballad, containing
as it does a chronicle of a certain well-defined transaction;
and the story of *King Canute* is a ballad—one of the best
that has been produced in our language in modern years.
But such pieces as those called *The End of the Play* and
Vanitas Vanitatum, which are didactic as well as pathetic,
are not ballads in the common sense; nor are such songs
as *The Mahogany Tree*, or the little collection called *Love
Songs made Easy*. The majority of the pieces are not
ballads; but if they be good of the kind, we should be
ungrateful to quarrel much with the name.

How very good most of them are, I did not know till I re-read them for the purpose of writing this chapter. There is a manifest falling off in some few—which has come from that source of literary failure which is now so common. If a man write a book or a poem because it is in him to write it—the motive power being altogether in himself, and coming from his desire to express himself— he will write it well, presuming him to be capable of the effort. But if he write his book or poem simply because a book or poem is required from him, let his capability be what it may, it is not unlikely that he will do it badly. Thackeray occasionally suffered from the weakness thus produced. A ballad from *Policeman X—Bow Street Ballads* they were first called—was required by *Punch*, and had to be forthcoming, whatever might be the poet's humour, by a certain time. *Jacob Omnium's Hoss* is excellent. His heart and feeling were all there, on behalf of his friend, and against that obsolete old court of justice. But we can tell well when he was looking through the police reports for a subject, and taking what chance might send him, without any special interest in the matter. *The Knight and the Lady of Bath*, and the *Damages Two Hundred Pounds*, as they were demanded at Guildford, taste as though they were written to order.

Here, in his verses as in his prose, the charm of Thackeray's work lies in the mingling of humour with pathos and indignation. There is hardly a piece that is not more or less funny, hardly a piece that is not satirical;—and in most of them, for those who will look a little below the surface, there is something that will touch them. Thackeray, though he rarely uttered a word, either with his pen or his mouth, in which there was not an intention to reach our sense of humour, never was only funny. When he

was most determined to make us laugh, he had always a
further purpose; some pity was to be extracted from us
on behalf of the sorrows of men, or some indignation at
the evil done by them.

This is the beginning of that story as to the *Two Hundred Pounds*, for which, as a ballad, I do not care very
much :

> Special jurymen of England who admire your country's laws,
> And proclaim a British jury worthy of the nation's applause,
> Gaily compliment each other at the issue of a cause,
> Which was tried at Guildford 'sizes, this day week as ever was.

Here he is indignant, not only in regard to some miscar-
riage of justice on that special occasion, but at the general unfitness of jurymen for the work confided to them.
"Gaily compliment yourselves," he says, "on your beautiful constitution, from which come such beautiful results
as those I am going to tell you !"   When he reminded
us that Ivanhoe had produced Magna Charta, there was a
purpose of irony even there in regard to our vaunted freedom.   With all your Magna Charta and your juries, what
are you but snobs !   There is nothing so often misguided
as general indignation, and I think that in his judgment
of outside things, in the measure which he usually took of
them, Thackeray was very frequently misguided.   A satirist by trade will learn to satirise everything, till the light
of the sun and the moon's loveliness will become evil and
mean to him.   I think that he was mistaken in his views
of things.   But we have to do with him as a writer, not
as a political economist or a politician.   His indignation
was all true, and the expression of it was often perfect.
The lines in which he addresses that Pallis Court, at the
end of *Jacob Omnium's Hoss*, are almost sublime.

168   THACKERAY.   [CHAP.

O Pallis Court, you move
  My pity most profound.
A most amusing sport
  You thought it, I'll be bound,
To saddle hup a three-pound
      debt,
  With two-and-twenty pound.

Good sport it is to you
  To grind the honest poor,
To pay their just or unjust debts
  With eight hundred per cent.,
      for Lor;
Make haste and get your costes in,
  They will not last much mor!

Come down from that tribewn,
  Thou shameless and unjust;
Thou swindle, picking pockets in
  The name of Truth august;
Come down, thou hoary Blas-
      phemy,
  For die thou shalt and must.

And go it, Jacob Homnium,
  And ply your iron pen,
And rise up, Sir John Jervis,
  And shut me up that den;
That sty for fattening lawyers
      in,
  On the bones of honest men.

"Come down from that tribewn, thou shameless and unjust!" It is impossible not to feel that he felt this as he wrote it.

There is a branch of his poetry which he calls — or which at any rate is now called, *Lyra Hybernica,* for which no doubt *The Groves of Blarney* was his model. There have been many imitations since, of which perhaps Barham's ballad on the coronation was the best, "When to Westminster the Royal Spinster and the Duke of Leinster all in order did repair!" Thackeray, in some of his attempts, has been equally droll and equally graphic. That on *The Cristal Palace* — not that at Sydenham, but its forerunner, the palace of the Great Exhibition — is very good, as the following catalogue of its contents will show:

There's holy saints
And window paints,
  By Maydiayval Pugin;
Alhamborough Jones
Did paint the tones
  Of yellow and gambouge in.

There's fountains there
And crosses fair;
  There's water-gods with urns;
There's organs three,
To play, d'ye see?
  "God save the Queen," by turns

There's statues bright
Of marble white,
  Of silver, and of copper;
And some in zinc,
And some, I think,
    That isn't over proper.

There's staym ingynes,
That stands in lines,
    Enormous and amazing,
That squeal and snort
Like whales in sport,
    Or elephants a grazing.

There's carts and gigs,
And pins for pigs,
  There's dibblers and there's
    harrows,

And ploughs like toys
For little boys,
    And ilegant wheel-barrows.

For thim genteels
Who ride on wheels,
    There's plenty to indulge 'em;
There's droskys snug
From Paytersbug,
    And vayhycles from Bulgium.

There's cabs on stands
And shandthry danns;
    There's waggons from New
      York here;
There's Lapland sleighs
Have crossed the seas,
    And jaunting cyars from Cork
      here.

In writing this Thackeray was a little late with his copy
for *Punch;* not, we should say, altogether an uncommon
accident to him. It should have been with the editor early on Saturday, if not before, but did not come till late on
Saturday evening. The editor, who was among men the
most good-natured, and I should think the most forbear-
ing, either could not, or in this case would not, insert it in
the next week's issue, and Thackeray, angry and disgusted,
sent it to *The Times.* In *The Times* of next Monday it
appeared—very much, I should think, to the delight of the
readers of that august newspaper.

Mr. Molony's account of the ball given to the Nepau-
lese ambassadors by the Peninsular and Oriental Company, is so like Barham's coronation in the account it
gives of the guests, that one would fancy it must be by
the same hand.

8*

The noble Chair[1] stud at the stair
    And bade the dhrums to thump; and he
Did thus evince to that Black Prince
    The welcome of his Company.[2]

O fair the girls and rich the curls,
    And bright the oys you saw there was;
And fixed each oye you then could spoi
    On General Jung Bahawther was!

This gineral great then tuck his sate,
    With all the other ginerals,
Bedad his troat, his belt, his coat,
    All bleezed with precious minerals;
And as he there, with princely air,
    Recloinin on his cushion was,
All round about his royal chair
    The squeezin and the pushin was.

O Pat, such girls, such jukes and earls,
    Such fashion and nobilitee!
Just think of Tim, and fancy him
    Amidst the high gentilitee!
There was the Lord de L'Huys, and the Portygeese
    Ministher and his lady there,
And I recognised, with much surprise,
    Our messmate, Bob O'Grady, there.

All these are very good fun—so good in humour and so good in expression, that it would be needless to criticise their peculiar dialect, were it not that Thackeray has made for himself a reputation by his writing of Irish. In this he has been so entirely successful that for many English readers he has established a new language which may not improperly be called Hybernico-Thackerayan. If comedy is to be got from peculiarities of dialect, as no doubt it is,

---

[1] Chair—*i. e.*, Chairman.   [2] *I. e.*, The P. and O. Company.

one form will do as well as another, so long as those who
read it know no better.   So it has been with Thackeray's
Irish, for in truth he was not familiar with the modes of
pronunciation which make up Irish brogue.   Therefore,
though he is always droll, he is not true to nature.   Many
an Irishman coming to London, not unnaturally tries to
imitate the talk of Londoners.   You or I, reader, were we
from the West, and were the dear County Galway to send
either of us to Parliament, would probably endeavour to
drop the dear brogue of our country, and in doing so we
should make some mistakes.   It was these mistakes which
Thackeray took for the natural Irish tone.   He was
amused to hear a major called "Meejor," but was una-
ware that the sound arose from Pat's affection of English
softness of speech.   The expression natural to the unadul-
terated Irishman would rather be "Ma-ajor."   He discov-
ers his own provincialism, and trying to be polite and ur-
bane, he says "Meejor."   In one of the lines I have quoted
there occurs the word "troat."   Such a sound never came
naturally from the mouth of an Irishman.   He puts in an
h instead of omitting it, and says "dhrink."   He comes
to London, and finding out that he is wrong with his
"dhrink," he leaves out all the h's he can, and thus comes
to "troat."   It is this which Thackeray has heard.   There
is a little piece called the *Last Irish Grievance*, to which
Thackeray adds a still later grievance, by the false sounds
which he elicits from the calumniated mouth of the
pretended Irish poet.   Slaves are "sleeves," places are
"pleeces," Lord John is "Lard Jahn," fatal is "fetal,"
danger is "deenger," and native is "neetive."   All these
are unintended slanders.   Tea, Hibernicé, is "tay," please
is "plaise," sea is "say," and ease is "aise."   The softer
sound of e is broadened out by the natural Irishman—not,

M   12

to my ear, without a certain euphony; but no one in Ireland says or hears the reverse. The Irishman who in London might talk of his "neetive" race, would be mincing his words to please the ear of the cockney.

The Chronicle of the Drum would be a true ballad all through, were it not that there is tacked on to it a long moral in an altered metre. I do not much value the moral, but the ballad is excellent, not only in much of its versification and in the turns of its language, but in the quaint and true picture it gives of the French nation. The drummer, either by himself or by some of his family, has drummed through a century of French battling, caring much for his country and its glory, but understanding nothing of the causes for which he is enthusiastic. Whether for King, Republic, or Emperor, whether fighting and conquering or fighting and conquered, he is happy as long as he can beat his drum on a field of glory. But throughout his adventures there is a touch of chivalry about our drummer. In all the episodes of his country's career he feels much of patriotism and something of tenderness. It is thus he sings during the days of the Revolution:

> We had taken the head of King Capet,
>   We called for the blood of his wife;
> Undaunted she came to the scaffold,
>   And bared her fair neck to the knife.
> As she felt the foul fingers that touched her,
>   She shrank, but she deigned not to speak;
> She looked with a royal disdain,
>   And died with a blush on her cheek!
>
> 'Twas thus that our country was saved!
>   So told us the Safety Committee!
> But, psha, I've the heart of a soldier—
>   All gentleness, mercy, and pity.

I loathed to assist at such deeds,
    And my drum beat its loudest of tunes,
As we offered to justice offended,
    The blood of the bloody tribunes.

Away with such foul recollections !
    No more of the axe and the block.
I saw the last fight of the sections,
    As they fell 'neath our guns at St. Rock.
Young Bonaparte led us that day.

And so it goes on.   I will not continue the stanza, because it contains the worst rhyme that Thackeray ever
permitted himself to use.   *The Chronicle of the Drum* has
not the finish which he achieved afterwards, but it is full
of national feeling, and carries on its purpose to the end
with an admirable persistency:

A curse on those British assassins
    Who ordered the slaughter of Ney;
A curse on Sir Hudson who tortured
    The life of our hero away.
A curse on all Russians—I hate them;
    On all Prussian and Austrian fry;
And, oh, but I pray we may meet them
    And fight them again ere I die.

The White Squall—which I can hardly call a ballad,
unless any description of a scene in verse may be included
in the name—is surely one of the most graphic descriptions ever put into verse.   Nothing written by Thackeray
shows more plainly his power over words and rhymes.
He draws his picture without a line omitted or a line
too much, saying with apparent facility all that he has to
say, and so saying it that every word conveys its natural
meaning.

When a squall, upon a sudden,
    Came o'er the waters scudding;

And the clouds began to gather,
And the sea was lashed to lather,
And the lowering thunder grumbled,
And the lightning jumped and tumbled,
And the ship and all the ocean
Woke up in wild commotion.
Then the wind set up a howling,
And the poodle-dog a yowling,
And the cocks began a crowing,
And the old cow raised a lowing,
As she heard the tempest blowing;
And fowls and geese did cackle,
And the cordage and the tackle
Began to shriek and crackle;
And the spray dashed o'er the funnels,
And down the deck in runnels;
And the rushing water soaks all,
From the seamen in the fo'ksal
To the stokers whose black faces
Peer out of their bed-places;
And the captain, he was bawling,
And the sailors pulling, hauling,
And the quarter-deck tarpauling
Was shivered in the squalling;
And the passengers awaken,
Most pitifully shaken;
And the steward jumps up and hastens
For the necessary basins.

Then the Greeks they groaned and quivered
And they knelt, and moaned, and shivered,
As the plunging waters met them,
And splashed and overset them;
And they call in their emergence
Upon countless saints and virgins;
And their marrowbones are bended,
And they think the world is ended.
And the Turkish women for'ard
Were frightened and behorror'd;

And shrieking and bewildering,
The mothers clutched their children;
The men sang "Allah! Illah!
Mashallah Bis-millah!"
As the warning waters doused them,
And splashed them and soused them;
And they called upon the Prophet,
And thought but little of it.

Then all the fleas in Jewry
Jumped up and bit like fury;
And the progeny of Jacob
Did on the main-deck wake up.
(I wot these greasy Rabbins
Would never pay for cabins);
And each man moaned and jabbered in
His filthy Jewish gaberdine,
In woe and lamentation,
And howling consternation.
And the splashing water drenches
Their dirty brats and wenches;
And they crawl from bales and benches,
In a hundred thousand stenches.
This was the White Squall famous,
Which latterly o'ercame us.

Peg of Limavaddy has always been very popular, and
the public have not, I think, been generally aware that the
young lady in question lived in truth at Newton Limavady
(with one d). But with the correct name Thackeray would
hardly have been so successful with his rhymes.

Citizen or Squire
    Tory, Whig, or Radi-
Cal would all desire
    Peg of Limavaddy.
Had I Homer's fire
    Or that of Sergeant Taddy

Meetly I'd admire
    Peg of Limavaddy.
And till I expire
    Or till I go mad I
Will sing unto my lyre
    Peg of Limavaddy.

The Cane-botiomed Chair is another, better, I think, than *Peg of Limavaddy*, as containing that mixture of burlesque with the pathetic which belonged so peculiarly to Thackeray, and which was indeed the very essence of his genius.

But of all the cheap treasures that garnish my nest,
    There's one that I love and I cherish the best.
For the finest of couches that's padded with hair
    I never would change thee, my cane-bottomed chair.

'Tis a bandy-legged, high-bottomed, worm-eaten seat,
    With a creaking old back and twisted old feet;
But since the fair morning when Fanny sat there,
    I bless thee and love thee, old cane-bottomed chair.

*   *   *   *   *

She comes from the past and revisits my room,
    She looks as she then did, all beauty and bloom;
So smiling and tender, so fresh and so fair,
    And yonder she sits in my cane-bottomed chair.

This, in the volume which I have now before me, is followed by a picture of Fanny in the chair, to which I cannot but take exception. I am quite sure that when Fanny graced the room and seated herself in the chair of her old bachelor friend, she had not on a low dress and loosely-flowing drawing-room shawl, nor was there a footstool ready for her feet. I doubt also the headgear. Fanny on that occasion was dressed in her morning apparel, and had walked through the streets, carried no fan, and wore no brooch but one that might be necessary for pinning her shawl.

The Great Cossack Epic is the longest of the ballads. It is a legend of St. Sophia of Kioff, telling how Father Hyacinth, by the aid of St. Sophia, whose wooden statue he carried with him, escaped across the Borysthenes with all the Cossacks at his tail. It is very good fun, but not equal to many of the others. Nor is the *Carmen Lilliense* quite to my taste. I should not have declared at once that it had come from Thackeray's hand, had I not known it.

But who could doubt the *Bouillabaisse?* Who else could have written that? Who at the same moment could have been so merry and so melancholy—could have gone so deep into the regrets of life, with words so appropriate to its jollities? I do not know how far my readers will agree with me that to read it always must be a fresh pleasure; but in order that they may agree with me, if they can, I will give it to them entire. If there be one whom it does not please, he will like nothing that Thackeray ever wrote in verse.

THE BALLAD OF BOUILLABAISSE.

A street there is in Paris famous,
    For which no rhyme our language yields,
Rue Neuve des Petits Champs its name is—
    The New Street of the Little Fields;
And here's an inn, not rich and splendid,
    But still in comfortable case;
The which in youth I oft attended,
    To eat a bowl of Bouillabaisse.

This Bouillabaisse a noble dish is—
    A sort of soup, or broth, or brew,
Or hotch-potch of all sorts of fishes,
    That Greenwich never could outdo;

Green herbs, red peppers, mussels, saffron,
    Soles, onions, garlic, roach, and dace :
All these you eat at Terré's tavern,
    In that one dish of Bouillabaisse.

Indeed, a rich and savoury stew 'tis ;
    And true philosophers, methinks,
Who love all sorts of natural beauties,
    Should love good victuals and good drinks.
And Cordelier or Benedictine
    Might gladly sure his lot embrace,
Nor find a fast-day too afflicting
    Which served him up a Bouillabaisse.

I wonder if the house still there is ?
    Yes, here the lamp is, as before ;
The smiling red-cheeked écaillère is
    Still opening oysters at the door.
Is Terré still alive and able ?
    I recollect his droll grimace ;
He'd come and smile before your table,
    And hope you liked your Bouillabaisse.

We enter—nothing's changed or older.
    "How's Monsieur Terré, waiter, pray ?"
The waiter stares and shrugs his shoulder—
    "Monsieur is dead this many a day."
"It is the lot of saint and sinner ;
    So honest Terré's run his race."
"What will Monsieur require for dinner ?"
    "Say, do you still cook Bouillabaisse ?"

"Oh, oui, Monsieur," 's the waiter's answer,
    "Quel vin Monsieur desire-t-il ?"
"Tell me a good one."   "That I can, sir :
    The chambertin with yellow seal."
"So Terré's gone," I say, and sink in
    My old accustom'd corner-place ;
"He's done with feasting and with drinking,
    With Burgundy and Bouillabaisse."

My old accustomed corner here is,
    The table still is in the nook;
Ah! vanish'd many a busy year is
    This well-known chair since last I took.
When first I saw ye, cari luoghi,
    I'd scarce a beard upon my face,
And now a grizzled, grim old fogy,
    I sit and wait for Bouillabaisse.

Where are you, old companions trusty,
    Of early days here met to dine?
Come, waiter! quick, a flagon crusty;
    I'll pledge them in the good old wine.
The kind old voices and old faces
    My memory can quick retrace;
Around the board they take their places,
    And share the wine and Bouillabaisse.

There's Jack has made a wondrous marriage;
    There's laughing Tom is laughing yet;
There's brave Augustus drives his carriage;
    There's poor old Fred in the *Gazette;*
O'er James's head the grass is growing.
    Good Lord! the world has wagged apace
Since here we set the claret flowing,
    And drank, and ate the Bouillabaisse.

Ah me! how quick the days are flitting!
    I mind me of a time that's gone,
When here I'd sit, as now I'm sitting,
    In this same place—but not alone.
A fair young face was nestled near me,
    A dear, dear face looked fondly up,
And sweetly spoke and smiled to cheer me?
    There's no one now to share my cup.

      *   *   *   *   *

I drink it as the Fates ordain it.
    Come fill it, and have done with rhymes;
Fill up the lonely glass, and drain it
    In memory of dear old times.

Welcome the wine, whate'er the seal is;
    And sit you down and say your grace
With thankful heart, whate'er the meal is.
    Here comes the smoking Bouillabaisse.

I am not disposed to say that Thackeray will hold a
high place among English poets. He would have been
the first to ridicule such an assumption made on his behalf. But I think that his verses will be more popular
than those of many highly reputed poets, and that as
years roll on they will gain rather than lose in public
estimation.

CHAPTER IX.

THACKERAY'S STYLE AND MANNER OF WORK.

A NOVEL in style should be easy, lucid, and of course grammatical. The same may be said of any book; but that which is intended to recreate should be easily understood—for which purpose lucid narration is an essential. In matter it should be moral and amusing. In manner it may be realistic, or sublime, or ludicrous; or it may be all these if the author can combine them. As to Thackeray's performance in style and matter I will say something further on. His manner was mainly realistic, and I will therefore speak first of that mode of expression which was peculiarly his own.

Realism in style has not all the ease which seems to belong to it. It is the object of the author who affects it so to communicate with his reader that all his words shall seem to be natural to the occasion. We do not think the language of Dogberry natural, when he tells neighbour Seacole that "to write and read comes by nature." That is ludicrous. Nor is the language of Hamlet natural when he shows to his mother the portrait of his father:

> See what a grace was seated on this brow;
> Hyperion's curls; the front of Jove himself;
> An eye like Mars, to threaten and command.

That is sublime. Constance is natural when she turns away from the Cardinal, declaring that

> He talks to me that never had a son.

In one respect both the sublime and ludicrous are easier than the realistic. They are not required to be true. A man with an imagination and culture may feign either of them without knowing the ways of men. To be realistic you must know accurately that which you describe. How often do we find in novels that the author makes an attempt at realism and falls into a bathos of absurdity, because he cannot use appropriate language? "No human being ever spoke like that," we say to ourselves—while we should not question the naturalness of the production, either in the grand or the ridiculous.

And yet in very truth the realistic must not be true— but just so far removed from truth as to suit the erroneous idea of truth which the reader may be supposed to entertain. For were a novelist to narrate a conversation between two persons of fair but not high education, and to use the ill-arranged words and fragments of speech which are really common in such conversations, he would seem to have sunk to the ludicrous, and to be attributing to the interlocutors a mode of language much beneath them. Though in fact true, it would seem to be far from natural. But, on the other hand, were he to put words grammatically correct into the mouths of his personages, and to round off and to complete the spoken sentences, the ordinary reader would instantly feel such a style to be stilted and unreal. This reader would not analyse it, but would in some dim but sufficiently critical manner be aware that his author was not providing him with a naturally spoken dialogue. To produce the desired effect the narrator must go be tween the two. He must mount somewhat above the ordinary conversational powers of such persons as are to be represented—lest he disgust. But he must by no means soar into correct phraseology—lest he offend. The realistic—by which we mean that which shall seem to be real —lies between the two, and in reaching it the writer has not only to keep his proper distance on both sides, but has to maintain varying distances in accordance with the position, mode of life, and education of the speakers. Lady Castlewood in *Esmond* would not have been properly made to speak with absolute precision; but she goes nearer to the mark than her more ignorant lord, the viscount; less near, however, than her better-educated kinsman, Henry Esmond. He, however, is not made to speak altogether by the card, or he would be unnatural. Nor would each of them speak always in the same strain, but they would alter their language according to their companion—according even to the hour of the day. All this the reader unconsciously perceives, and will not think the language to be natural unless the proper variations be there.

In simple narrative the rule is the same as in dialogue, though it does not admit of the same palpable deviation from correct construction. The story of any incident, to be realistic, will admit neither of sesquipedalian grandeur nor of grotesque images. The one gives an idea of romance and the other of burlesque, to neither of which is truth supposed to appertain. We desire to soar frequently, and then we try romance. We desire to recreate ourselves with the easy and droll. Dulce est desipere in loco. Then we have recourse to burlesque. But in neither do we expect human nature.

I cannot but think that in the hands of the novelist the middle course is the most powerful. Much as we may delight in burlesque, we cannot claim for it the power of achieving great results. So much, I think, will be granted. For the sublime we look rather to poetry than to prose; and though I will give one or two instances just now in which it has been used with great effect in prose fiction, it does not come home to the heart, teaching a lesson, as does the realistic. The girl who reads is touched by Lucy Ashton, but she feels herself to be convinced of the facts as to Jeanie Deans, and asks herself whether she might not emulate them.

Now as to the realism of Thackeray, I must rather appeal to my readers than attempt to prove it by quotation. Whoever it is that speaks in his pages, does it not seem that such a person would certainly have used such words on such an occasion? If there be need of examination to learn whether it be so or not, let the reader study all that falls from the mouth of Lady Castlewood through the novel called *Esmond*, or all that falls from the mouth of Beatrix. They are persons peculiarly situated — noble women, but who have still lived much out of the world. The former is always conscious of a sorrow; the latter is always striving after an effect—and both on this account are difficult of management. A period for the story has been chosen which is strange and unknown to us, and which has required a peculiar language. One would have said beforehand that whatever might be the charms of the book, it would not be natural. And yet the ear is never wounded by a tone that is false. It is not always the case that in novel reading the ear should be wounded because the words spoken are unnatural. Bulwer does not wound, though he never puts into the mouth of any of his persons words such as would have been spoken. They are not expected from him. It is something else that he provides.

From Thackeray they are expected—and from many others. But Thackeray never disappoints. Whether it be a great duke, such as he who was to have married Beatrix, or a mean chaplain, such as Tusher, or Captain Steele the humorist, they talk—not as they would have talked probably, of which I am no judge—but as we feel that they might have talked. We find ourselves willing to take it as proved because it is there, which is the strongest possible evidence of the realistic capacity of the writer.

As to the sublime in novels, it is not to be supposed that any very high rank of sublimity is required to put such works within the pale of that definition. I allude to those in which an attempt is made to soar above the ordinary actions and ordinary language of life. We may take as an instance *The Mysteries of Udolpho*. That is intended to be sublime throughout. Even the writer never for a moment thought of descending to real life. She must have been untrue to her own idea of her own business had she done so. It is all stilted — all of a certain altitude among the clouds. It has been in its time a popular book, and has had its world of readers. Those readers no doubt preferred the diluted romance of Mrs. Radcliff to the condensed realism of Fielding. At any rate, they did not look for realism. *Pelham* may be taken as another instance of the sublime, though there is so much in it that is of the world worldly, though an intentional fall to the ludicrous is often made in it. The personages talk in glittering dialogues, throwing about philosophy, science, and the classics, in a manner which is always suggestive and often amusing. The book is brilliant with intellect. But no word is ever spoken as it would have been spoken—no detail is ever narrated as it would have occurred. Bulwer no doubt regarded novels as romantic, and would have looked

9

with contempt on any junction of realism and romance, though, in varying his work, he did not think it beneath him to vary his sublimity with the ludicrous. The sublime in novels is no doubt most effective when it breaks out, as though by some burst of nature, in the midst of a story true to life. "If," said Evan Maccombich, "the Saxon gentlemen are laughing because a poor man such as me thinks my life, or the life of six of my degree, is worth that of Vich Ian Vohr, it's like enough they may be very right; but if they laugh because they think I would not keep my word and come back to redeem him, I can tell them they ken neither the heart of a Hielandman nor the honour of a gentleman." That is sublime. And, again, when Balfour of Burley slaughters Bothwell, the death scene is sublime. "Die, bloodthirsty dog!" said Burley. "Die as thou hast lived! Die like the beasts that perish—hoping nothing, believing nothing!"—"And fearing nothing," said Bothwell. Horrible as is the picture, it is sublime. As is also that speech of Meg Merrilies, as she addresses Mr. Bertram, standing on the bank. "Ride your ways," said the gipsy; "ride your ways, Laird of Ellangowan; ride your ways, Godfrey Bertram. This day have ye quenched seven smoking hearths; see if the fire in your ain parlour burn the blyther for that. Ye have riven the thack off seven cottar houses; look if your ain roof-tree stand the faster. Ye may stable your stirks in the shealings at Derncleugh; see that the hare does not couch on the hearthstane at Ellangowan." That is romance, and reaches the very height of the sublime. That does not offend, impossible though it be that any old woman should have spoken such words, because it does in truth lift the reader up among the bright stars. It is thus that the sublime may be mingled with the realistic, if the writer has the power. Thackeray also rises in that way to a high pitch, though not in many instances. Romance does not often justify to him an absence of truth. The scene between Lady Castlewood and the Duke of Hamilton is one when she explains to her child's suitor who Henry Esmond is. "My daughter may receive presents from the head of our house," says the lady, speaking up for her kinsman. "My daughter may thankfully take kindness from her father's, her mother's, her brother's dearest friend." The whole scene is of the same nature, and is evidence of Thackeray's capacity for the sublime. And again, when the same lady welcomes the same kinsman on his return from the wars, she rises as high. But as I have already quoted a part of the passage in the chapter on this novel, I will not repeat it here.

It may perhaps be said of the sublime in novels—which I have endeavoured to describe as not being generally of a high order—that it is apt to become cold, stilted, and unsatisfactory. What may be done by impossible castles among impossible mountains, peopled by impossible heroes and heroines, and fraught with impossible horrors, *The Mysteries of Udolpho* have shown us. But they require a patient reader, and one who can content himself with a long protracted and most unemotional excitement. The sublimity which is effected by sparkling speeches is better, if the speeches really have something in them beneath the sparkles. Those of Bulwer generally have. Those of his imitators are often without anything, the sparkles even hardly sparkling. At the best they fatigue; and a novel, if it fatigues, is unpardonable. Its only excuse is to be found in the amusement it affords. It should instruct also, no doubt, but it never will do so unless it hides its instruction and amuses. Scott understood all this, when

N   13

he allowed himself only such sudden bursts as I have de-scribed. Even in *The Bride of Lammermoor,* which I do not regard as among the best of his performances, as he soars high into the sublime, so does he descend low into the ludicrous.

In this latter division of pure fiction—the burlesque, as it is commonly called, or the ludicrous — Thackeray is quite as much at home as in the realistic, though, the ve-hicle being less powerful, he has achieved smaller results by it. Manifest as are the objects in his view when he wrote *The Hoggarty Diamond* or *The Legend of the Rhine,* they were less important and less evidently effected than those attempted by *Vanity Fair* and *Pendennis.* Cap-tain Shindy, the Snob, does not tell us so plainly what is not a gentleman as does Colonel Newcome what is. Nev-ertheless, the ludicrous has, with Thackeray, been very powerful and very delightful.

In trying to describe what is done by literature of this class, it is especially necessary to remember that different readers are affected in a different way. That which is one man's meat is another man's poison. In the sublime, when the really grand has been reached, it is the reader's own fault if he be not touched. We know that many are indifferent to the soliloquies of Hamlet, but we do not hesitate to declare to ourselves that they are so because they lack the power of appreciating grand language. We do not scruple to attribute to those who are indifferent some inferiority of intelligence. And in regard to the realistic, when the truth of a well-told story or life-like character does not come home, we think that then, too, there is deficiency in the critical ability. But there is nothing necessarily lacking to a man because he does not enjoy *The Heathen Chinee* or *The Biglow Papers;* and the man to whom these delights of American humour are leather and prunello may be of all the most enraptured by the wit of Sam Weller or the mock piety of Pecksniff. It is a matter of taste and not of intellect, as one man likes caviare after his dinner, while another prefers apple-pie ; and the man himself cannot, or, as far as we can see, does not, direct his own taste in the one matter more than in the other.

Therefore I cannot ask others to share with me the delight which I have in the various and peculiar expressions of the ludicrous which are common to Thackeray. Some considerable portion of it consists in bad spelling. We may say that Charles James Harrington Fitzroy Yellowplush, or C. FitzJeames De La Pluche, as he is afterwards called, would be nothing but for his "orthogwaphy so carefully inaccuwate." As I have before said, Mrs. Malaprop had seemed to have reached the height of this humour, and in having done so to have made any repetition unpalatable. But Thackeray's studied blundering is altogether different from that of Sheridan. Mrs. Malaprop uses her words in a delightfully wrong sense. Yellowplush would be a very intelligible, if not quite an accurate writer, had he not made for himself special forms of English words altogether new to the eye.

"My ma wrapped up my buth in a mistry. I may be illygitmit; I may have been changed at nus ; but I've always had gen'l'm'nly tastes through life, and have no doubt that I come of a gen'l'm'nly origum." We cannot admit that there is wit, or even humour, in bad spelling alone. Were it not that Yellowplush, with his bad spelling, had so much to sa ' for himself, there would be nothing in it; but there is always a sting of satire directed against some real vice, or ome growing vulgarity, which is made sharper by the absurdity of the language. In *The Diary of George IV.* there are the following reflections on a certain correspondence : " Wooden you phansy, now, that the author of such a letter, instead of writun about pipple of tip-top quality, was describin' Vinegar Yard ? Would you beleave that the lady he was a-ritin' to was a chased modist lady of honour and mother of a family ? *O trumpery ! o morris !* as Homer says. This is a higeous pictur of manners, such as I weap to think of, as every morl man must weap." We do not wonder that when he makes his " ajew " he should have been called up to be congratulated on the score of his literary performances by his master, before the Duke, and Lord Bagwig, and Dr. Larner, and " Sawedwadgeorgeearllittnbulwig." All that Yellowplush says or writes are among the pearls which Thackeray was continually scattering abroad.

But this of the distinguished footman was only one of the forms of the ludicrous which he was accustomed to use in the furtherance of some purpose which he had at heart. It was his practice to clothe things most revolting with an assumed grace and dignity, and to add to the weight of his condemnation by the astounding mendacity of the parody thus drawn. There was a grim humour in this which has been displeasing to some, as seeming to hold out to vice a hand which has appeared for too long a time to be friendly. As we are disposed to be not altogether sympathetic with a detective policeman who shall have spent a jolly night with a delinquent, for the sake of tracing home the suspected guilt to his late comrade, so are some disposed to be almost angry with our author, who seems to be too much at home with his rascals, and to live with them on familiar terms till we doubt whether he does not forget their rascality. *Barry Lyndon* is the strongest example we have of this style of the ludicrous, and the critics of whom I speak have thought that our friendly relations with Barry have been too genial, too apparently genuine, so that it might almost be doubtful whether during the narrative we might not, at this or the other crisis, be rather with him than against him. "After all," the reader might say, on coming to that passage in which Barry defends his trade as a gambler—a passage which I have quoted in speaking of the novel—"after all, this man is more hero than scoundrel;" so well is the burlesque humour maintained, so well does the scoundrel hide his own villany. I can easily understand that to some it should seem too long drawn out. To me it seems to be the perfection of humour—and of philosophy. If such a one as Barry Lyndon, a man full of intellect, can be made thus to love and cherish his vice, and to believe in its beauty, how much more necessary is it to avoid the footsteps which lead to it? But, as I have said above, there is no standard by which to judge of the excellence of the ludicrous as there is of the sublime, and even the realistic.

No writer ever had a stronger proclivity towards parody than Thackeray; and we may, I think, confess that there is no form of literary drollery more dangerous. The parody will often mar the gem of which it coarsely reproduces the outward semblance. The word "damaged," used instead of "damask," has destroyed to my ear for ever the music of one of the sweetest passages in Shakespeare. But it must be acknowledged of Thackeray that, fond as he is of this branch of humour, he has done little or no injury by his parodies. They run over with fun, but are so contrived that they do not lessen the flavour of the original. I have given in one of the preceding chap' ters a little set of verses of his own, called *The Willow Tree*, and his own parody on his own work. There the reader may see how effective a parody may be in destroying the sentiment of the piece parodied. But in dealing with other authors he has been grotesque without being severely critical, and has been very like, without making ugly or distasteful that which he has imitated. No one who has admired *Coningsby* will admire it the less because of *Codlingsby*. Nor will the undoubted romance of *Eugene Aram* be lessened in the estimation of any reader of novels by the well-told career of *George de Barnwell*. One may say that to laugh *Ivanhoe* out of face, or to lessen the glory of that immortal story, would be beyond the power of any farcical effect. Thackeray, in his *Rowena and Rebecca*, certainly had no such purpose. Nothing of *Ivanhoe* is injured, nothing made less valuable than it was before, yet, of all prose parodies in the language, it is perhaps the most perfect. Every character is maintained, every incident has a taste of Scott. It has the twang of *Ivanhoe* from beginning to end, and yet there is not a word in it by which the author of *Ivanhoe* could have been offended. But then there is the purpose beyond that of the mere parody. Prudish women have to be laughed at, and despotic kings, and parasite lords and bishops. The ludicrous alone is but poor fun ; but when the ludicrous has a meaning, it can be very effective in the hands of such a master as this.

" He to die !" resumed the bishop. " He a mortal like to us !
Death was not for him intended, though *communis omnibus*.
Keeper, you are irreligious, for to talk and cavil thus !"

So much I have said of the manner in which Thackeray did his work, endeavouring to represent human nature as he saw it, so that his readers should learn to love what is good, and to hate what is evil. As to the merits of his style, it will be necessary to insist on them the less, because it has been generally admitted to be easy, lucid, and grammatical. I call that style easy by which the writer has succeeded in conveying to the reader that which the reader is intended to receive with the least possible amount of trouble to him. I call that style lucid which conveys to the reader most accurately all that the writer wishes to convey on any subject. The two virtues will, I think, be seen to be very different. An author may wish to give an idea that a certain flavour is bitter. He shall leave a conviction that it is simply disagreeable. Then he is not lucid. But he shall convey so much as that, in such a manner as to give the reader no trouble in arriving at the conclusion. Therefore he is easy. The subject here suggested is as little complicated as possible; but in the intercourse which is going on continually between writers and readers, affairs of all degrees of complication are continually being discussed, of a nature so complicated that the inexperienced writer is puzzled at every turn to express himself, and the altogether inartistic writer fails to do so. Who among writers has not to acknowledge that he is .often unable to tell all that he has to tell? Words refuse to do it for him. He struggles and stumbles and alters and adds, but finds at last that he has gone either too far or not quite far enough. Then there comes upon him the necessity of choosing between two evils. He must either give up the fulness of his thought, and content himself with presenting some fragment of it in that lucid arrangement of words which he affects; or he must bring out his thought with ambages; he must mass his sentences inconsequentially; he must struggle up hill almost

9*

hopelessly with his phrases—so that at the end the reader will have to labour as he himself has laboured, or else to leave behind much of the fruit which it has been intended that he should garner. It is the ill-fortune of some to be neither easy or lucid; and there is nothing more wonderful in the history of letters than the patience of readers when called upon to suffer under the double calamity. It is as though a man were reading a dialogue of Plato, understanding neither the subject nor the language. But it is often the case that one has to be sacrificed to the other. The pregnant writer will sometimes solace himself by declaring that it is not his business to supply intelligence to the reader; and then, in throwing out the entirety of his thought, will not stop to remember that he cannot hope to scatter his ideas far and wide unless he can make them easily intelligible. Then the writer who is determined that his book shall not be put down because it is troublesome, is too apt to avoid the knotty bits and shirk the rocky turns, because he cannot with ease to himself make them easy to others. If this be acknowledged, I shall be held to be right in saying not only that ease and lucidity in style are different virtues, but that they are often opposed to each other. They may, however, be combined, and then the writer will have really learned the art of writing. Omne tulit punctum qui miscuit utile dulci. It is to be done, I believe, in all languages. A man by art and practice shall at least obtain such a masterhood over words as to express all that he thinks, in phrases that shall be easily understood.

In such a small space as can here be allowed, I cannot give instances to prove that this has been achieved by Thackeray. Nor would instances prove the existence of the virtue, though instances might the absence. The proof lies in the work of the man's life, and can only become plain to those who have read his writings. I must refer readers to their own experiences, and ask them whether they have found themselves compelled to study passages in Thackeray in order that they might find a recondite meaning, or whether they have not been sure that they and the author have together understood all that there was to understand in the matter. Have they run backward over the passages, and then gone on, not quite sure what the author has meant? If not, then he has been easy and lucid. We have not had it so easy with all modern writers, nor with all that are old. I may best, perhaps, explain my meaning by taking something written long ago; something very valuable, in order that I may not damage my argument by comparing the easiness of Thackeray with the harshness of some author who has in other respects failed of obtaining approbation. If you take the play of *Cymbeline*, you will, I think, find it to be anything but easy reading. Nor is Shakespeare always lucid. For purposes of his own he will sometimes force his readers to doubt his meaning, even after prolonged study. It has ever been so with *Hamlet*. My readers will not, I think, be so crossgrained with me as to suppose that I am putting Thackeray as a master of style above Shakespeare. I am only endeavouring to explain by reference to the great master the condition of literary production which he attained. Whatever Thackeray says, the reader cannot fail to understand; and whatever Thackeray attempts to communicate, he succeeds in conveying.

That he is grammatical I must leave to my readers' judgment, with a simple assertion in his favour. There are some who say that grammar — by which I mean accuracy of composition, in accordance with certain acknowl-

edged rules — is only a means to an end; and that, if a
writer can absolutely achieve the end by some other mode
of his own, he need not regard the prescribed means.   If
a man can so write as to be easily understood, and to
convey lucidly that which he has to convey without accuracy of grammar, why should he subject himself to unnecessary trammels?   Why not make a path for himself,
if the path so made will certainly lead him whither he
wishes to go?   The answer is, that no other path will
lead others whither he wishes to carry them but that
which is common to him and to those others.   It is necessary that there should be a ground equally familiar to
the writer and to his readers.   If there be no such common ground, they will certainly not come into full accord.
There have been recusants who, by a certain acuteness of
their own, have partly done so — wilful recusants; but
they have been recusants, not to the extent of discarding
grammar—which no writer could do and not be altogether
in the dark—but so far as to have created for themselves
a phraseology which has been picturesque by reason of its
illicit vagaries; as a woman will sometimes please ill-in-
structed eyes and ears by little departures from feminine
propriety.   They have probably laboured in their vocation
as sedulously as though they had striven to be correct,
and have achieved at the best but a short-lived success—
as is the case also with the unconventional female.   The
charm of the disorderly soon loses itself in the ugliness of
disorder.   And there are others rebellious from grammar,
who are, however, hardly to be called rebels, because the
laws which they break have never been altogether known
to them.   Among those very dear to me in English literature, one or two might be named of either sort, whose
works, though they have that in them which will insure to

them a long life, will become from year to year less valuable and less venerable, because their authors have either
scorned or have not known that common ground of language on which the author and his readers should stand
together. My purport here is only with Thackeray, and I
say that he stands always on that common ground. He
quarrels with none of the laws. As the lady who is most
attentive to conventional propriety may still have her own
fashion of dress and her own mode of speech, so had
Thackeray very manifestly his own style; but it is one
the correctness of which has never been impugned.

I hold that gentleman to be the best dressed whose
dress no one observes. I am not sure but that the same
may be said of an author's written language. Only, where
shall we find an example of such perfection ? Always
easy, always lucid, always correct, we may find them; but
who is the writer, easy, lucid, and correct, who has not
impregnated his writing with something of that personal
flavour which we call mannerism ? To speak of authors
well known to all readers—Does not *The Rambler* taste of
Johnson ; *The Decline and Fall*, of Gibbon ; *The Middle
Ages*, of Hallam ; *The History of England*, of Macaulay ;
and *The Invasion of the Crimea*, of Kinglake ? Do we
not know the elephantine tread of *The Saturday*, and the
precise toe of *The Spectator ?* I have sometimes thought
that Swift has been nearest to the mark of any—writing
English and not writing Swift. But I doubt whether an
accurate observer would not trace even here the "mark
of the beast." Thackeray, too, has a strong flavour of
Thackeray. I am inclined to think that his most beset-
ting sin in style—the little ear-mark by which he is most
conspicuous—is a certain affected familiarity. He indulges too frequently in little confidences with individual

readers, in which pretended allusions to himself are fre-
quent. "What would you do? what would you say now,
if you were in such a position?" he asks. He describes
this practice of his in the preface to *Pendennis*. "It is a
sort of confidential talk between writer and reader. . . .
In the course of his volubility the perpetual speaker must
of necessity lay bare his own weaknesses, vanities, peculiarities." In the short contributions to periodicals on which
he tried his 'prentice hand, such addresses and conversations were natural and efficacious; but in a larger work of
fiction they cause an absence of that dignity to which even
a novel may aspire. You feel that each morsel as you
read it is a detached bit, and that it has all been written
in detachments. The book is robbed of its integrity by a
certain good-humoured geniality of language, which causes
the reader to be almost too much at home with his author. There is a saying that familiarity breeds contempt,
and I have been sometimes inclined to think that our author has sometimes failed to stand up for himself with
sufficiency of "personal deportment."

In other respects Thackeray's style is excellent. As I
have said before, the reader always understands his words
without an effort, and receives all that the author has to
give.

There now remains to be discussed the matter of our
author's work. The manner and the style are but the
natural wrappings in which the goods have been prepared
for the market. Of these goods it is no doubt true that
unless the wrappings be in some degree meritorious the
article will not be accepted at all; but it is the kernel
which we seek, which, if it be not of itself sweet and di-
gestible, cannot be made serviceable by any shell, however
pretty or easy to be cracked. I have said previously that

it is the business of a novel to instruct in morals and to amuse. I will go further, and will add, having been for many years a most prolific writer of novels myself, that I regard him who can put himself into close communication with young people year after year without making some attempt to do them good as a very sorry fellow indeed. However poor your matter may be, however near you may come to that "foolishest of existing mortals," as Carlyle presumes some unfortunate novelist to be, still, if there be those who read your works, they will undoubtedly be more or less influenced by what they find there. And it is because the novelist amuses that he is thus influential. The sermon too often has no such effect, because it is applied with the declared intention of having it. The palpable and overt dose the child rejects; but that which is cunningly insinuated by the aid of jam or honey is accepted unconsciously, and goes on upon its curative mission. So it is with the novel. It is taken because of its jam and honey. But, unlike the honest simple jam and honey of the household cupboard, it is never unmixed with physic. There will be the dose within it, either curative or poisonous. The girl will be taught modesty or immodesty, truth or falsehood; the lad will be taught honour or dishonour, simplicity or affectation. Without the lesson the amusement will not be there. There are novels which certainly can teach nothing; but then neither can they amuse any one.

I should be said to insist absurdly on the power of my own confraternity if I were to declare that the bulk of the young people in the upper and middle classes receive their moral teaching chiefly from the novels they read. Mothers would no doubt think of their own sweet teaching; fathers of the examples which they set; and schoolmas-

ters of the excellence of their instructions.   Happy is the
country that has such mothers, fathers, and schoolmasters!
But the novelist creeps in closer than the schoolmaster,
closer than the father, closer almost than the mother.   He
is the chosen ·guide, the tutor whom the young pupil
chooses for herself.   She retires with him, suspecting no
lesson, safe against rebuke, throwing herself head and heart
into the narration as she can hardly do into her task-work;
and there she is taught—how she shall learn to love; how
she shall receive the lover when he comes; how far she
should advance to meet the joy; why she should be reticent, and not' throw herself at once into this new delight.
It is the same with the young man, though he would be
more prone even than she to reject the suspicion of such
tutorship.   But he too will there learn either to speak the
truth, or to lie; and will receive from his novel lessons either of real manliness, or of that affected apishness and
tailor-begotten demeanour which too many professors of
the craft give out as their dearest precepts.

At any rate the close intercourse is admitted.   Where
is the house now from which novels are tabooed?   Is it
not common to allow them almost indiscriminately, so that
young and old each chooses his own novel?   Shall he,
then, to whom this close fellowship is allowed—this inner
confidence—shall he not be careful what words he uses,
and what thoughts he expresses, when he sits in council
with his young friend?   This, which it will certainly be
his duty to consider with so much care, will be the matter
of his work.   We know what was thought of such matter
when Lydia in the play was driven to the necessity of
flinging "*Peregrine Pickle* under the toilet," and thrust-
ing "*Lord Aimwell* under the sofa."   We have got beyond that now, and are tolerably sure that our girls do not

hide their novels. The more freely they are allowed, the more necessary is it that he who supplies shall take care that they are worthy of the trust that is given to them.

Now let the reader ask himself what are the lessons which Thackeray has taught. Let him send his memory running back over all those characters of whom we have just been speaking, and ask himself whether any girl has been taught to be immodest, or any man unmanly, by what Thackeray has written. A novelist has two modes of teaching—by good example or bad. It is not to be supposed that because the person treated of be evil, therefore the precept will be evil. If so, some personages with whom we have been made well acquainted from our youth upwards would have been omitted in our early lessons. It may be a question whether the teaching is not more efficacious which comes from the evil example. What story was ever more powerful in showing the beauty of feminine reticence, and the horrors of feminine evil-doing, than the fate of Effie Deans? The Templar would have betrayed a woman to his lust, but has not encouraged others by the freedom of his life. Varney was utterly bad—but though a gay courtier, he has enticed no others to go the way that he went. So it has been with Thackeray. His examples have been generally of that kind—but they have all been efficacious in their teaching on the side of modesty and manliness, truth and simplicity. When some girl shall have traced from first to last the character of Beatrix, what, let us ask, will be the result on her mind? Beatrix was born noble, clever, beautiful, with certain material advantages, which it was within her compass to improve by her nobility, wit, and beauty. She was quite alive to that fact, and thought of those material advantages, to the utter exclusion, in our mind, of any idea of moral goodness.

he realised it all, and told herself that that was the game she would play. " Twenty-five !" says she ; " and in eight years no man has ever touched my heart !" That is her boast when she is about to be married—her only boast of herself. " A most detestable young woman !" some will say. " An awful example !" others will add. Not a doubt of it. She proves the misery of her own career so fully that no one will follow it. The example is so awful that it will surely deter. The girl will declare to herself that not in that way will she look for the happiness which she hopes to enjoy ; and the young man will say, as he reads it, that no Beatrix shall touch his heart.

You may go through all his characters with the same effect. Pendennis will be scorned because he is light; Warrington loved because he is strong and merciful ; Dobbin will be honoured because he is unselfish ; and the old colonel, though he be foolish, vain, and weak, almost worshipped because he is so true a gentleman. It is in the handling of questions such as these that we have to look for the matter of the novelist—those moral lessons which he mixes up with his jam and his honey. I say that with Thackeray the physic is always curative and never poisonous. He may be admitted safely into that close fellowship, and be allowed to accompany the dear ones to their retreats. The girl will never become bold under his preaching, or taught to throw herself at men's heads. Nor will the lad receive a false flashy idea of what becomes a youth, when he is first about to take his place among men.

As to that other question, whether Thackeray be amusing as well as salutary, I must leave it to public opinion. There is now being brought out of his works a more splendid edition than has ever been produced in any age or any country of the writings of such an author. A certain fixed number of copies only is being issued, and each copy will cost £33 12s. when completed. It is understood that a very large proportion of the edition has been already bought or ordered. Cost, it will be said, is a bad test of excellence. It will not prove the merit of a book any more than it will of a horse. But it is proof of the popularity of the book. Print and illustrate and bind up some novels how you will, no one will buy them. Previous to these costly volumes, there have been two entire editions of his works since the author's death, one comparatively cheap and the other dear. Before his death his stories had been scattered in all imaginable forms. I may therefore assert that their charm has been proved by their popularity.

There remains for us only this question—whether the nature of Thackeray's works entitle him to be called a cynic. The word is one which is always used in a bad sense. "Of a dog; currish," is the definition which we get from Johnson—quite correctly, and in accordance with its etymology. And he gives us examples. "How vilely does this cynic rhyme," he takes from Shakespeare; and Addison speaks of a man degenerating into a cynic. That Thackeray's nature was soft and kindly—gentle almost to a fault—has been shown elsewhere. But they who have called him a cynic have spoken of him merely as a writer —and as writer he has certainly taken upon himself the special task of barking at the vices and follies of the world around him. Any satirist might in the same way be called a cynic in so far as his satire goes. Swift was a cynic, certainly. Pope was cynical when he was a satirist. Juvenal was all cynical, because he was all satirist. If that be what is meant, Thackeray was certainly a cynic. But that is not all that the word implies. It intends to go back beyond the work of the man, and to describe his

O   14

heart. It says of any satirist so described that he has given himself up to satire, not because things have been evil, but because he himself has been evil. Hamlet is a satirist, whereas Thersites is a cynic. If Thackeray be judged after this fashion, the word is as inappropriate to the writer as to the man.

But it has to be confessed that Thackeray did allow his intellect to be too thoroughly saturated with the aspect of the ill side of things. We can trace the operation of his mind from his earliest days, when he commenced his parodies at school; when he brought out *The Snob* at Cambridge, when he sent *Yellowplush* out upon the world as a satirist on the doings of gentlemen generally; when he wrote his *Catherine*, to show the vileness of the taste for what he would have called Newgate literature; and *The Hoggarty Diamond*, to attack bubble companies; and *Barry Lyndon*, to expose the pride which a rascal may take in his rascality. Becky Sharp, Major Pendennis, Beatrix, both as a young and as an old woman, were written with the same purpose. There is a touch of satire in every drawing that he made. A jeer is needed for something that is ridiculous, scorn has to be thrown on something that is vile. The same feeling is to be found in every line of every ballad.

VANITAS VANITATUM.

Methinks the text is never stale,
    And life is every day renewing
Fresh comments on the old old tale,
    Of Folly, Fortune, Glory, Ruin.

Hark to the preacher, preaching still!
    He lifts his voice and cries his sermon,
Here at St. Peter's of Cornhill,
    As yonder on the Mount of Hermon—

> For you and me to heart to take
> (O dear beloved brother readers),
> To-day—as when the good king spake
> Beneath the solemn Syrian cedars.

It was just so with him always. He was "crying his sermon," hoping, if it might be so, to do something towards lessening the evils he saw around him. We all preach our sermon, but not always with the same earnestness. He had become so urgent in the cause, so loud in his denunciations, that he did not stop often to speak of the good things around him. Now and again he paused and blessed amid the torrent of his anathemas. There are Dobbin, and Esmond, and Colonel Newcome. But his anathemas are the loudest. It has been so, I think, nearly always with the eloquent preachers.

I will insert here — especially here at the end of this chapter, in which I have spoken of Thackeray's matter and manner of writing, because of the justice of the criticism conveyed—the lines which Lord Houghton wrote on his death, and which are to be found in the February number of *The Cornhill* of 1864. It was the first number printed after his death. I would add that, though no Dean applied for permission to bury Thackeray in Westminster Abbey, his bust was placed there without delay. What is needed by the nation in such a case is simply a lasting memorial there, where such memorials are most often seen and most highly honoured. But we can all of us sympathise with the feeling of the poet, writing immediately on the loss of such a friend :

> When one, whose nervous English verse
> Public and party hates defied,
> Who bore and bandied many a curse
> Of angry times—when Dryden died,

Our royal abbey's Bishop-Dean
 Waited for no suggestive prayer,
But, ere one day closed o'er the scene,
 Craved, as a boon, to lay him there.

The wayward faith, the faulty life,
 Vanished before a nation's pain.
Panther and Hind forgot their strife,
 And rival statesmen thronged the fane.

O gentle censor of our age!
 Prime master of our ampler tongue!
Whose word of wit and generous page
 Were never wrath, except with wrong,—

Fielding—without the manner's dross,
 Scott—with a spirit's larger room,
What Prelate deems thy grave his loss?
 What Halifax erects thy tomb?

But, may be, he—who so could draw
 The hidden great—the humble wise,
Yielding with them to God's good law,
 Makes the Pantheon where he lies.

THE END.

ENGLISH MEN OF LETTERS.

EDITED BY JOHN MORLEY.

12mo, Cloth, 75 cents per Volume.
Also, People's Edition (36 volumes in 12), 12mo, Cloth, $1 00 per volume.
Other Volumes in Preparation.

PUBLISHED BY HARPER & BROTHERS, NEW YORK.

☞ *Any of the above works will be sent by mail, postage prepaid, to any part of the United States, Canada, or Mexico, on receipt of the price.*

A NEW LIBRARY EDITION

OF

MACAULAY'S ENGLAND.

MACAULAY'S HISTORY OF ENGLAND. New Edition, from New Electrotype Plates. 5 volumes, 8vo, Cloth, with Paper Labels, Gilt Tops and Uncut Edges, $10 00; Sheep, $12 50; Half Calf, $21 25. *Sold only in Sets.*

The beauty of the edition is the beauty of proper workmanship and solid worth—the beauty of fitness alone. Nowhere is the least effort made to decorate the volumes externally or internally. They are perfectly printed from new plates that have been made in the best manner, and with the most accurate understanding of what is needed; and they are solidly bound, with absolutely plain black cloth covers, without relief of any kind, except such as is afforded by the paper label. It is a set of plain, solid, sensible volumes, made for use, and so made as to be comfortable in the using.— *N. Y. Evening Post.*

OTHER EDITIONS OF MACAULAY'S ENGLAND.

LIBRARY EDITION: 5 volumes, 8vo, Cloth, $10 00.

POPULAR EDITION: 5 volumes, 12mo, Cloth, $2 50.

CHEAP EDITION: 5 volumes, 8vo, Paper, $1 00. In one volume, 8vo, Cloth, $1 25.

The volumes are sold separately.

Published by HARPER & BROTHERS, New York.

☞ *Sent by mail, postage prepaid, to any part of the United States, on receipt of the price.*